GOOD ENTERTAINMENT

UNTIMELY MEDITATIONS

GOOD ENTERTAINMENT

A DECONSTRUCTION OF THE WESTERN PASSION NARRATIVE

BYUNG-CHUL HAN

TRANSLATED BY ADRIAN NATHAN WEST

THE MIT PRESS
CAMBRIDGE, MASSACHUSETTS
LONDON, ENGLAND

This translation © 2019 Massachusetts Institute of Technology

Originally published as *Gute Unterhaltung. Eine Dekonstruktion der abendländischen Passionsgeschichte* in the series *Fröhliche Wissenschaft* by Matthes & Seitz Berlin: © Matthes & Seitz Berlin Verlagsgesellschaft mbH, Berlin 2016. All rights reserved.

This book was set in PF DinText Pro by Toppan Best-set Premedia Limited. Printed and bound in the United States of America.

Library of Congress Cataloging-in-Publication Data

Names: Han, Byung-Chul, author.
Title: Good entertainment : a deconstruction of the western passion narrative / Byung-Chul Han ; translated by Adrian Nathan West.
Other titles: Gute Unterhaltung. English
Description: Cambridge, MA : MIT Press, 2019. | Includes bibliographical references.
Identifiers: LCCN 2018059326 | ISBN 9780262537506 (pbk. : alk. paper)
Subjects: LCSH: Aesthetics, Modern. | Deconstruction. | Arts—Moral and ethical aspects. | Jesus Christ—Passion. | Amusement—Philosophy.
Classification: LCC BH151 .H2813 2019 | DDC 111/.85—dc23 LC record available at https://lccn.loc.gov/2018059326

10   9   8   7   6   5   4   3

CONTENTS

The history of the West is a passion narrative. Achievement is the new formula for passion. Passion makes its reappearance as a killjoy. In truth, work and play are mutually exclusive. But today, even play is being subordinated to production. It is being gamified.

The achievement society remains a society of passion. Even athletes dope themselves to achieve better performance. Something grotesque inheres in the entertainment that arises as an incidental corollary. It deteriorates into mental deactiviation. A definitive triumph over the age of passion will bring not only good entertainment, but also beautiful entertainment, that is, entertainment through beauty. PLAY will exist again.

PREFACE

Its character is *passion*. Music does not suffer in man, it does not partake of his dealings and his feelings: it suffers over him ... Music lays ... gently on his shoulders the suffering mandated by the stars above.
—Theodor W. Adorno

Writing as a form of prayer.
—Franz Kafka

Something fundamentally new is arising at present through the ubiquity of entertainment. A basic change is occurring in our understanding of the world and reality. Entertainment today is vaunted as a new paradigm, even a new credo for being, which decides what is and is not *apt for the world*, indeed, what *is*, period. In this way, *reality* appears as a characteristic *effect* of entertainment.

The totalization of entertainment leads to a hedonistic world that the spirit of passion interprets as, disparages as, abasement, invalidation, nonbeing. And yet, in their essence, passion and entertainment are not entirely different. The pure meaninglessness of entertainment is adjacent to the pure meaning of passion. The fool's smile bears a ghastly resemblance to the pain-racked visage of *Homo doloris*. The latter mortgages happiness for bliss. This paradox demands further exploration.

SWEET CROSS

By thee, source of all good things,
Much good has befallen me.
Thy mouth has refreshed me
With milk and sweetmeats.
Thy spirit has favored me
With many a heavenly longing.
—Johann Sebastian Bach, *Saint Matthew's Passion*

When *Saint Matthew's Passion* was first played in the Saint Thomas Church in Leipzig on Good Friday in 1727, all present were driven, according to reports from the time, into a state of "utmost astonishment." "Councilors and noble ladies looked at each other and said: 'What will come next?'" From horror, a pious widow shouted: "God help us, children! It is like being at an opera or a comedy!" This, according to a certain Christian Gerber in his *History of Church Ceremonies in Saxony*.[1] Gerber, who could easily have been a strict Kantian, decried the growing use of music in church services. He lamented the presence of "minds" that "from such vain natures" felt a pleasure that could be described as "sanguine and inclined to sensuality." *Music and passion cannot abide one another*: "As to whether moderate music has its place in the church ... as is well known, it is prone to excesses, and one would like to say, echoing Moses, Ye take too much upon you, Children of Levi, Numbers 16.18. For it often sounds worldly and lively, better suited to the dance floor or the opera than to worship. When sung in this way, music, to the thinking of many pious hearts, does not recall the passion in the least."[2]

The effect of *Saint Matthew's Passion* on the Leipzig notables must have been excessively theatrical and operatic. Its recital sharpened already existing tensions with Bach. The council resolved to cut his wages. In the contract Bach signed as *Thomaskantor*, it reads: "For the maintenance of good order, to provide music in the church that shall not last too long, and to perform it in such a way that its effects are not operatic, and it encourages silent devotion in the listener."[3] This curious proviso to the cantor's duties gives some sense of the growing hybridization of spiritual and secular music. Gradually, spiritual music was breaking from its liturgical context and coming to resemble bourgeois-modern concert music: "As traits of the 'theatrical' style of secular cantata and opera, which the Pietists ... roundly rejected, began to permeate religious music, a path opened up for musical form at the end of which beckoned the ideal of Gluck's opera and Haydn's oratorium."[4]

On one hand, Latinate airiness, sensual raptness, and lush, luxuriant melody play an increasingly decisive role in the musical life of Bach's era. "Connoisseurs" and "enthusiasts" make up the new music-consuming public. For them, appreciation consists primarily of enjoyment and the cultivation of taste. On the other hand, even in Lutheran Orthodox circles, critical voices rise up against the presence of art music in religious services. A strict antagonism to music emerges from the Pietist movement. Only devout songs with catchy melodies sung softly to oneself are to be tolerated. Music should not overwhelm the *word*, may not harbor any power of its own. Gerber refers back to Johann Conrad Dannhauer, the teacher of Philipp Jakob Spener, founder of Pietism: "We do not deem instrumental music anything more than an ornament of the church, extraneous to the essence of worship. This great theologian, too, rejects the imported custom of singing during instrumental music, as the lyrics are voiced in such a way that no one can properly understand them amid the booming and blaring of the instruments."[5] Resigned to the implacable diffusion of music in church, Gerber recommends to "good souls," his readers, that they "bear it with patience" and not let themselves be "disgusted" by religious services.[6]

Gerber would prefer that organs be banned from the church: "Nor is one organ sufficient, in many churches there must be two, and we are driven to ask: wherefore all this excess?"[7] The organ, according to Gerber, should be used for the sole purpose of setting the tone, so that songs will be sung through to the end: "Organs are in a certain way useful, serving to begin the song in the proper tone and to carry it through to the end. For it is quite common for the precentor, cantor, or schoolmaster to let the pitch drop, and then the hymn can barely be finished."[8] Here, the organ is stripped of any intrinsic aesthetic worth. The instrument's blaring is merely an obstacle to the comprehension of the text. Instrumental music would best be done away with in favor of the *word*: "religious services comprise prayer, singing, tribute, and heeding or contemplating the Word of God, and none of this has need of any musical instruments, which the early Christian church did without for two to three hundred years."[9]

Church music is a mere "ornament." It is *external* to the "essence of worship." Gerber invokes Theophil Großgebauer, whose basic hostility to music brings him close to the Pietists, citing his "Voice of a Guardian from Devastated Zion" (1661), a text rife with prophetic fervor: "The playing of music rather amuses the sentiments than inclines the heart inwardly toward things divine."[10] Music is the *external*, and the *internal* must be safeguarded from it: "Does the Savior not tell us clearly that the Kingdom of God comes not with observable signs, but instead lies within us?"[11] Here, music is reduced to a *garnish*, a "seasoning for the senses" inessential to the "authentic meal of the word," comparable to that "sugar" which "sweetens the divine medicine."[12]

The strict division between internal and external, heart and sentiment, essence and ornament, meal and seasoning, is problematic. Does seasoning not belong somehow to the essence of a meal? Might there not be a divine word that, instead of bitter "medicine," is *sweet* on its own? For God does reveal himself as the "highest sweetness" to the "taste" of the mystically inclined soul.[13] How ought one distinguish, then, between God's sweetness and the sweetness of music?

The Pietists were famously opposed to dancing. And yet, paradoxically, the melodies of their religious songs were strikingly similar to dance music. Some even sound like minuets. A self-proclaimed "lover of the pure gospel and friend of healthy theology" remarks sardonically that Pietist songs were "better suited to dancing than devotion," "drawing one forward, a new song is being sung, but to melodies from the days when grandfather used to grab grandmother by the hand."[14]

Against the "pomp and pageantry" that enchants the "poor folk," Großgebauer repeatedly stresses the primacy of the *word*.[15] God's word alone gives rise to divine joy. It is "wisdom," according to Großgebauer, "to bring God's word into comely psalms / and to send God's word in graceful melodies through the ear into the heart." No divine joy, in contrast, characterizes the "monstrous female goddess Cybele," who played "her music so ecstatically that she spilled her own blood."[16] The Phrygian mode, the mode of ecstasy and passion, is traceable to the orgiastic music of the Cybelian or Dionysian mysteries. For Großgebauer, Cybelian music in church services was to be avoided, being a goad to ecstasy and the forgetting of the word. Yet he does not strictly eschew drunkenness in all its forms. Instead, it crops up elsewhere. Like a "sweet wine," the psalms should make the "spirit" drunk: "Just as wine fills the drunkard / so must spirit fill the parish. What does the apostle hand us / that we may fill ourselves with spirit? Nothing but psalms / songs of praise, spirited chants. That is the sweet wine / the parish must drink / if it wishes to become full with spirit."[17] How, though, do we distinguish between the drunkenness of the spirit and that of the senses? Is there an essential difference between word- and music-drunkenness, between godly and worldly wine? God—is that a synonym for *absolute* delight?[18] The Pietist singer Anna Maria Schuchart, known for her ecstatic trances and visions, is said to have sung upon awakening from "the torpor of deep sleep":

> Soon mayst thou in heaven taste
> Eternally in grace
> Christ's blood
> For your good
> Flowing from Christ's wounds
> On his cross so roughly hewn.
> [...]
> Look on the comeliest joy
> That thou shalt graze upon in heaven.
> [...]
> When the world has descended
> To the abyss of Hell
> Christ most splendid
> With thee shall dwell,
> Abandon earth
> On his rebirth
> And don his crown
> In eternal bliss.[19]

According to Großgebauer, holy blood, the blood of Christ, must not be mingled with the blood of Cybele. And yet the taste of the one closely resembles that of the other. Both are sweet. And both inebriate.

Gerber calls advocates of art music in church "sanguine and inclined to sensuality." The librettist of *Saint Matthew's*

Passion, Christian Friedrich Henrici, whom Bach was said to be on good terms with, must himself have had a sanguine nature.[20] In the *Universal German Biography* (1880), one finds the following entry on Henrici: "Though not lacking in poetic talent ... he sought, through tasteless wit and coarse, immoral jokes ... to accommodate boorish souls, and succeeded superbly in doing so. His recompense for this was the contempt of the finer sort among his contemporaries, as well as of posterity." It goes on to say that his poems "abound" in "proverbial expressions, and occasionally the most uncommon ones," which are often "of an obscene nature."[21] It is this same Henrici, alias Picander, the man of obscene inclinations, who composed the libretto for *Saint Matthew's Passion*. He also wrote many of Bach's secular songs, among them the Coffee Cantata (BWV 211). Here Lieschen sings a *sensuous aria*:

> Ay! How sweet coffee tastes
> A thousand kisses would not be so fine,
> It is milder than muscat wine.
> I must have coffee, coffee;
> And if you wish to give me cheer,
> Well, then, bring a coffee here!

According to the *Universal German Biography*, Picander was far from a pious man. He must have viewed the contents of the passion story in a highly skeptical light. The sensuous aria from the cantata "Hercules at the Crossroads," which he also wrote the lyrics for, reads like a summary of his personal philosophy:

Who would choose sweat
When without a care
Nor a worry to spare
He may have his true salvation?

The legend "Anti-Melancholicus," which Bach appended to the inside cover of the piano booklet for his wife Anna Magdalena, could serve as a motto for his life. Bach must have had in mind a "happy *musicus*" relishing the "foretaste of heavenly delight." For this *musicus beautus*, entertainment or the delectation of the mind did not conflict with the praise of God.

In the *Generalbasslehre* (1738),[22] Bach gives a definition of the thoroughbass: "As with all music, so with the thoroughbass, the ultimate end and final goal is nothing more than the honor of God and recreation of the soul. Where this is not attended to, there is no true music, but rather a devilish blaring and racket."[23] For his thoroughbass treatise, Bach clearly relied on Friedrich Erhard Niedt's *Musical Guide* (1710) as a model. He does, however, make one significant departure from Niedt's definition of the thoroughbass. Niedt writes: "The ultimate end or final goal of all music, including thoroughbass, shall be nothing but the Honor of God and recreation of the soul. Where this is not attended to, there is no true music, and those who misuse this noble and divine art for the kindling of lust and carnal desires are musicians of the Devil. For Satan takes pleasure in listening to such shameful sounds. For him such music is good enough, but to the ears of God it is a disgraceful racket."[24] Bach's definition of the thoroughbass fails to clarify what transforms music into "devilish blaring and racket." Bach has omitted from Niedt's definition expressions like "lust" and "carnal desires." Perhaps he realized the experience of lust was integral to the delight of the spirit. As concerns music appreciation, it is hard to distinguish between heavenly and devilish pleasure, between divine and worldly delight. Moreover, not only "Satan" but also Jesus inspires lust. In Bach's spiritual cantata, lust stubbornly persists. The cantata "Behold, what love the Father has shown us" contains a *hymn to lust*:

> What should I ask of the world and its delights
> When you alone, my Jesus, are my light!
> You alone may quench my pleasure's thirst:
> You are my desire: what else should I ask of the earth!

On the title page of the *Little Organ Book* (1712–1717), the young Bach notes: "To God most high, whom I beseech / my fellow man His wisdom to teach." As yet there is no mention of the delectation of the mind. Music is, above all, a *laudatio Dei*. In the *Clavier Übung* of 1739, however, all talk God's honor has vanished. God yields to the delectation of the mind: "Third Part of Keyboard Practice, consisting of various preludes to the Catechism and other hymns for the organ: for the delight of the minds of music-lovers and particularly for connoisseurs of works of this sort." The *Goldberg Variations* (1741–42), composed for a count plagued with sleeplessness, bear the notice: "For the lovers of the delight of the mind." That his music is now addressed to lovers or connoisseurs places it fully outside the theological context, in which man takes pleasure in divine order, a divine harmony of the world that music mirrors. Music now serves for the cultivation of taste and for enjoyment. In this sense it is manifestly modern.

Could Bach not also have prefaced his *Saint Matthew's Passion* with the remark: "for the delight of the minds of music-lovers and particularly for connoisseurs of works of this sort"? *Saint Matthew's Passion* is distinguished by extraordinary dramatic tension. Dialogues give its sections the character of theatrical scenes. And so the pious widow's protestation is not entirely exaggeration: "God help us, children! It is like being at an opera or a comedy!"

Bach's *Saint Matthew's Passion* was long forgotten. Not until one hundred years later, on March 11, 1829, was it restaged by Mendelssohn in Berlin: not in a church, not during religious services, but rather in a concert hall. Significantly, Paganini gave a concert that same day in Berlin. Mendelssohn's changes leave Bach's *Passion*, in a certain way, poor in *words*.[25] He has struck out biblical passages, eliminated elements that might impede dramatic progression. The work was shortened to half of its original performance time. Hurried tempos were introduced, along with protracted crescendos that heightened the suspense. The dry recitative "And Behold, the Veil of the Temple Is Rent," in which the dramatic events subsequent to Christ's crucifixion are accompanied by a lone keyboard, is imbued with new color, and transformed into a sumptuous aural painting.[26] In contrast, the chorale "If I Must One Day Depart," which precedes this recitative Mendelssohn orchestrated, is now sung a cappella, offering a contrast that draws out

SWEET CROSS

the emotion of the scene.[27] Even more than its predecessor, this lyrical-romantic version of the *Saint Matthew's Passion* merits the addendum: "For lovers of the delight of the mind."

In 1870 the young Friedrich Nietzsche wrote to his friend Erwin Rohde from Basel: "This week I have heard *three times* the divine Bach's the *Saint Matthew's Passion*, each time with the same feeling of immeasurable wonder. Whoever has fully unlearned Christianity hears it here truthfully as a gospel: this is the music of the negation of the will, without any remembrance of asceticism."[28] In later years, however, the enlightened Nietzsche would come to perceive in Bach's music "an excess of crude Christianity," "crude Germanness," and "crude Scholasticism." Bach may well stand at the threshold of modern music, which, according to Nietzsche, had conquered the "church" and "counterpoint." But upon this threshold, Bach turns back to the Middle Ages.[29]

Whoever has fully unlearned Christianity will not regain his faith with the aid of passion music, which at most *dances around* the resulting *vacuum* with tones and feelings. God here becomes a *theatrical effect*, at most a *sound effect* or a *property of counterpoint* that will dissolve no sooner than the music has died away. Friedrich Schleiermacher, who along with Georg Wilhelm Friedrich Hegel and Heinrich Heine attended the Berlin revival of *Saint Matthew's Passion*, must have embraced this *aural reminiscence* of the divine, which only disclosed itself to feeling. As a *concept*, the religious content is eroded. The religion of art or of art music presupposes the decay of religion as such. What is left, when the *signifier* or the *word* "God" is vacated? Does passion not finally dovetail into *recreation*, the entertainment of the mind?

Even as a pious fourteen-year-old, Nietzsche is already pondering modern music. The central purpose of modern music is to "guide our thoughts to things higher, uplift us." This is eminently the purpose of church music. Music ought not be employed for amusement. "Almost the entirety of modern music," however, bears "traces of this." Nietzsche draws an analogy between modern music and the "poetry of the future" and that youth which as yet lacks "thoughts of its own," and attempts to "conceal its absence of ideas behind a dazzling, glimmering style." Modern music produces only a *beautiful semblance* without any deeper meaning.[30]

The later Nietzsche, on the other hand, will celebrate "lightness," "youth," and "gaiety." This is not a sublime gaiety, edged with sorrow, as we find in Martin Heidegger, but rather a gaiety that is "African."[31] "Il faut," Nietzsche writes, "méditerraniser la musique." He forswears Wagnerian music, which "*sweats*" and so is tantamount to a kind of *passion*—even more so because, inevitably, it aims for "redemption": "Wagner has contemplated nothing so deeply as redemption: his opera is the opera of redemption."[32] The music of youth, of "health" and of "nature," on the other hand, is a music of gaiety, of sweet *being here*, requiring no redemption, no rescue. Nietzsche enthuses over a "Moorish dance," over music with a "southern, brown, burnt sensibility," for the "yellow afternoon of its happiness," which is "brief, sudden, unforgiving." He praises that music which "arises" "softly, pliantly, with politeness."[33] The "first principle" of his aesthetics runs: "What is good is light; whatever is divine moves on tender feet." Wagner's music, on the other hand, Nietzsche portrays as a pressing, torrid southeasterly wind, a "sirocco": "I break out into a disagreeable sweat. *My* good weather is gone." Moreover, writes Nietzsche, the new music is "popular." It is not the music "of an individual," but rather "popular" music, even *pop music* with an "African" groove.

Nietzsche contrasts Offenbach's "lightness" with the "heavy," "deep" "pathos" of Wagner. Offenbach's music, "free" and "bright," emerging with a light step, promises a "proper redemption from the maudlin and ultimately degenerate music of the German Romantics"; a peculiar redemption, then, a redemption from the incessant demand for redemption.[34] It dwells in *contented being here.* Offenbach's "levity," his "buoyancy," redeems music from *passion*, from the "unwillingness to let go of an extreme feeling."[35] Music of this sort, without "pathos," without the "appalling longueur" of pathos, would be a watchword for freedom, a music for *homines liberi et hilari.* Here Nietzsche takes leave of *Homo doloris.*

A strict division between redemption and delight, between passion and entertainment, is equally untenable in the case of Bach, whether on the musical plane or on the textual or conceptual one. "Cheer" oscillates between God, the gums, and the genitals. Unrequited "lust" returns by backroads to the domain of the sacred. Not only "coffee" and "kisses" are "sweet," but the "cross" as well. "Sweet cross" is not an oxymoron, but a pleonasm. "Jesus, your passion is a pure joy to me," as the *Saint John Passion* says. Redemption transforms even death into "sweet heavenly joy." No strict division is possible between "heavenly pleasure" and the "delight of the mind" attributable to the *name*, the *signifier* "God." This instead functions as a focal point, bundling and intensifying joy and pleasure and, in this way, safeguarding them from *diffusion*.

In *Laws*, Plato draws a firm distinction between various forms of music and expressly proscribes their intermingling. He forbids the mixing of hymns, songs addressed to the gods, and other, secular music. He condemns those poets who blend everything together and are led "unintentionally to slander their profession by the assumption that in music there is no such thing as right and wrong, the right standard of judgment being the pleasure given to the hearer, high or low."[36] According to Plato, the honor of God and the delight of the mind are fundamentally distinct and not to be combined. The law is responsible for ensuring their strict separation.

Bach would not follow Plato's mandate concerning the upholding of music's purity. Even his parody procedure involves a merging of spiritual and secular music. Repeatedly, Bach inserts sections of secular cantatas in his spiritual compositions. His Christmas Oratorio contains excerpts of the "dramma per musica" *Hercules at the Crossroads*. This musical drama shows Hercules's heroic resistance to the allurements of satanic "lust." As the hero holds out against "sweet temptation," he swears fidelity to virtue.

Lust:
Sleep, my beloved, and be at ease,
Let the temptations of lusty thoughts guide you.
　　Taste the savor
　　Of sensual nature
　　And let no chains confine you.
[...]
Hercules:
I hear you not, I know you not,
Spurned lust, you are a stranger.
　　For the snakes
　　That sought to take
　　Me in my boyhood I have long since caught and strangled.
Beloved virtue, none but you
Shall be my guide
Ever at my side.

Later, Bach resurrects this aria of satanic lust in the *Christmas Oratorio* as a lullaby for Jesus. The composition of another text, however, will serve as the basis of his parody procedure. Seen in this way, "Lied zur Ruhe" depicts not Satanic lust, which Jesus must defy for the sake of virtue or the redemption of humankind, but rather invokes a sweet pleasure the child may yield to without resistance:

Go there, shepherds, go,
That you may see the miracle and know
The son of the Lord most high; be led
and when you find him in his meager bed

Speak to him in dulcet tones
Rock his crib, and all as one
Sing this song to peace!
Sleep, my dear, enjoy your rest,
Let this pleasure swell your breast,
Wake to this resounding voice,
Be blissful as our hearts rejoice!

On the musical plane, at least, Bach's parody procedure permits the total fusion of God with pleasure. There is something strange in an imperative of this kind addressed to Jesus: "Let this pleasure swell your breast, / Wake to this resounding voice, / Be blissful as our hearts rejoice!" Over and over, the original aria of unfettered lust rings through: "Taste the savor / Of sensual nature / And let no chains confine you!" Through parody, Bach incorporates lust, however unconsciously, into the narrative of salvation and passion. Even *Saint Matthew's Passion* closes not with a frightful song, but with a sweet one. After his passion, Jesus falls asleep "in utmost bliss." The refrain, "My Jesus, good night!" gives the closing section of *Saint Matthew's Passion* the air of a lullaby, a song of valediction, which seems to hail another time, another *being here* that has no further need of redemption:

My Jesus, good night!
[...]
My Jesus, good night!
[...]
Rest softly, softly rest!
Rest, you weary limbs!

Rest softly, rest well.
The grave where you dwell
Like a cushion will console
The heavy, fearful head,
For the body grant a bed,
And a shelter for the soul.
And the joyous eyes, unencumbered,
Now delight in their slumber.[37]

BUTTERFLY DREAMS

Sometimes, with extremely long pieces, I used to feel like I was playing a Gameboy. I would get lost in Mozart, would hop around inside, like I was playing Chinese jump rope, and with Tchaikovsky I discovered a passion not so different from making a run for the opposing team's goal.

—Lang Lang

In *Travel Pictures*, Heinrich Heine lavishes praise on the music of Gioachino Rossini. He invokes the golden tones, the melodic flashes, the butterfly dreams "that so beguile him."[1] His heart is kissed "as if by the lips of the graces." Heine calls Rossini *divino maestro*, the Helios of Italy. He casts his "sonorous beams" down over the world. He flutters lightly, as if given wings by God. Heine begs Rossini to forgive his poor compatriots, who fail to grasp his depths because they are covered over with roses. In Hell, Heine affirms, they will not evade their deserved reprimand, and will be condemned to hear nothing but Bach's fugues for the length of eternity.

It is well known that not everyone praised Rossini so enthusiastically. For many, he was synonymous with frivolity and light entertainment. Robert Schumann called him a "decorative painter" whose melodic flourishes and ornamentation aimed no higher than sensuous enjoyment, a mindless, truthless intoxication of the senses. His music was a fleeting butterfly dream, a beautiful illusion that fell apart completely when stripped of its "deceptive theatrical distance."[2] Rossini's compositions were sumptuously ornamented frames that lacked a picture capable of *expressing* a thought or idea. E. T. A. Hoffmann speaks of the "sweet, Rossinian lemonade" that "art-savorers" "slurp down without the slightest complaint."[3] He contrasts this with the "fiery, strong, potent wine of a great dramatic composer." Rossini, according to Hoffmann "careless, and therefore unworthy of true art," indulges "faddish tastes." Hoffmann wonders: "How can it be ... that even in Germany, where otherwise only truth and seriousness matter in art, this decadent taste finds such a multitude of adherents?"

The dichotomy of seriousness versus entertainment is already crucial in music criticism of the nineteenth century. In Wendt's biography of Rossini (1824) we read: "In the first place, he satisfies the ear, working for a sweet, charming music. ... He has always had the *greater public*—not the critics—in mind; the *effect* was ever his God, and the easier it was for him to earn acclaim by means of it, the more enthusiastically and recklessly he pursued it, with disregard for serious artistic practice."[4] Rossini's music is portrayed as *popular* music that bows down before the taste of the masses.

Wagner, too, blames Rossini's musical faults on his excessive attention to his public.[5] For Wagner, the "distinguishing feature of the good" is that "it is there for itself" and requires no public. The "good in its pure form," which is only realized in the "work of a genius," stands aloof from the "demand for entertainment." The "bad in art" corresponds to the intention "simply to please." In his theory of art, Wagner posits a dichotomous tension that absolutizes or hierarchizes a putatively relative difference into an unyielding moral law. Wagner designates the "*good in art*" as a "*moral good*."[6] A sharp dichotomy of this kind generates an aura of *depth*. Its violation entails the dissipation of this aura.

An excess of pleasure in melodies, however seductive it may be, generates "disgust." The melodies themselves grow "suddenly unbearable," even "risible."[7] But was the "eerie splendor of [Beethoven's] stare, painfully broken, withered from longing—and yet undaunted unto death" not also, in the end, risible or comic?[8]

For Wagner, music is akin to poetry. It is fertilized by "the thoughts of the poet." True melody is suffused with words and meaning. Music is preeminently *expression*. Beethoven "throws himself" "into the arms of the poet" "in order to *beget* true melody, infallibly real and redemptive."[9] Where music is bare of expression, of the poetic word, of *passion*, it provokes "disgust."

A wholly different notion of music lies behind Arthur Schopenhauer's enthusiasm for Rossini. In *The World as Will and Representation*, he writes: "Thus if music ties itself too closely to words or tries to model itself on events, it is trying to speak a language that is not its own. Nobody has avoided this error as completely as *Rossini*: which is why his music speaks its *own* language so clearly and purely that it has no need of words at all and retains its full effect when performed on instruments alone."[10] In the opinion of an Italian contemporary, Rossini liberates music from the fetters of expression and thought. His music is therefore freer than that other music which is "paroxysm from the first to the last notes," and merely "harnesses" the text, offering nothing but a "fabric" of "thoughts and modulations" that "attack one another in the eardrum."[11] Hence the sardonic rhyme:

> Voici le mot; songez y bien;
> Crier est tout, chanter n'est rien.[12]

If music is conceived as something other than passion and expression, then Rossini's songs certainly sing more than that song "which is not song, but rather only an eternally unbroken longing to sing."[13] Viewed thus, Beethoven's *Fidelio*, which lacks free singing, is not opera, but simply "declamation set to instruments." Music "full of thrusting, leaping, moods, that is enraptured by the shifting storms of passion" lacks the freedom of "sustained, penetrating song." Hence Rossini's smile would have *a splendor of its own*, no less dignified than the splendor of Beethoven's painfully broken stare. Not only the face twisted in pain, but the serene smile would have *depth*, albeit a depth not apparent at first glance because, to quote Heine, it is covered with roses.

Rossini marks a contrast with that tragic hero who, while striving "to make the entire world his own," is laid low by his "enemy," that is, by "indomitable nature." Rossini succeeds in conquering the world, though his way of doing so is utterly different. His power is "pleasure," the "enchantment of melodies," which dominates by *gratifying*. A power that *entertains* is stronger than one that compels: "Submitting to the flights of his genius, he strives onward, never even conscious of a conquest so immense, it finds its counterpart in the fable of Orpheus. Pleasure is his helpmeet, nature his allied power."[14]

Rossini's music is free insofar as it is hostage neither to thoughts, nor to ideas, nor to words. When the German singers remarked that "the leaden nature of the German language made it impossible to clearly pronounce and appreciate the words at a rapid tempo," Rossini apparently shouted: "Che cosa? Parole? Effetto! Effetto!"[15] Often Rossini's melodies express nothing so much as that luxuriant, frolicking foliage Kant describes as "*free* beauty," because it depends on no thought or concept. Rossini's music hovers as though "given wings by God" because it is not freighted with that "appalling *longueur*" of "pathos" from which Nietzsche distances himself. Rossini's music is rife with tones that long for nothing, that require nothing, that have no need of redemption.

Being free from specific expression, his melodies achieve a *global* effect. His music thus becomes both *popular* and *global*.

Strange to each other in language, strange in customs
[...]
Are the Indian, the Mexican, and perhaps
Even the Hottentot and the Huron
Gripped by the exalted magic
Of Rossini's song? What new power
Is this? Wherefore sinks melody
So gladly into man's heart?[16]

Even Hegel allows himself to be carried away by Rossini's melodies. After hearing Rossini's *Barber of Seville* for the second time in Vienna, he wrote enthusiastically to his wife: "It is so glorious, so irresistible, that one cannot leave Vienna."[17] Hegel takes Rossini's side against his critics: "Rossini's detractors dismiss his music as empty titillation for the ears; but if one penetrates its melodies more deeply, this music is, to the contrary, replete with feeling, rich in spirit, a goad to the mind and heart."[18]

Hegel's enthusiasm for Rossini is less than self-evident in light of his asseveration that art that serves merely for "pleasure and entertainment" is "not independent, not free, but rather servile."[19] *"Free* art," in contrast, neither pleases nor entertains. It *works* toward the truth. Hegel's "spirit," as the subject of art, is itself *work and passion.* The relationship to truth and spirit forms the basis of the kinship between art and philosophy: "Now, in its freedom alone is fine art truly art, and it only fulfills its supreme task when it has placed itself in the same sphere as religion and philosophy, and when it is simply one way of bringing to our minds and expressing the *Divine,* the deepest interests of mankind, and the most comprehensive truths of the spirit."[20]

Hegel draws attention to the "conditions of our time," which "are not favorable to art." "Our life today," writes Hegel, is oriented to "general considerations" that exceed the scope of the art's domain, that is, the sensory. Whether from a deficit of generality or an excess of sensuality, art for us is "a thing of the past." For the contemporary frame of mind, it does not represent a medium of truth. "Thought" and "reflection" have, as Hegel remarks, "spread their wings" over fine art.[21] The site of passion or the work of the spirit has shifted to philosophy and science, which are more suited to knowledge and truth. Art does not work efficiently enough as it were, or else its products no longer satisfy the criteria of truth.

Art yields before science and philosophy, and at the same time is delivered from service to truth. De-passioned, it becomes the object either of "immediate enjoyment" or of scientific observation.[22] This de-passioning of art is what inspires in Hegel that carefree enthusiasm for Rossini's music. He forgets, for a moment, the *work for truth*, *thinking as passion*. He indulges in a very different passion, a passion for the beautiful, which is delightful to the degree that it is free from compulsion to meaning or truth, from any kind of work as passion. To his wife, Hegel writes from Prague: "I enjoy such beauty, and live in utopia."[23] Not knowledge and understanding, but rather the lack of meaning, leads to utopia.

"Utopia" does not form part of Hegel's philosophical vocabulary. Only once does he speak of the "ideal of a philosophical utopia." In doing so, he opposes the idea of an "originary truth" that "submits wholly to the passivity of thinking, which need only open its mouth to consume it completely."[24] Thinking, for Hegel, is work and passion. Knowledge is the result of "doing." It is hence anything but that strange "fruit" that falls from the "tree of knowledge," "already chewed and digested."

Awash in beauty, Hegel believes he dwells in utopia. Utopia is *absolute entertainment*. Pure happiness exists only where work comes to rest. Rossini's music, its "gratified tone," excites and cheers him, puts him in a utopian mood. His "melodic stream" is a "divine furor." It delights and liberates every situation.[25] Rossini's god bears no family resemblance to the god of Hegel. His is a *god of entertainment*, unworried by truth or the word. His god was the effect, as it was said. The god of entertainment and the god of passion, the god of pure effect and the god of pure truth, the god of pure melody and the god of the pure word, pure immanence, and pure transcendence are therefore closely allied.

The Greeks, according to Nietzsche, had a special inclination toward the word. Even when passion was played out on the stage, it was necessary that "it speak well."[26] A proclivity for the word is "unnatural" insofar as passion in nature is "so poor in words, so embarrassed, and all but mute." The Greeks reveled in this unnaturalness: "the tragic hero still finds words, reasons, eloquent gestures, and altogether intellectual brightness, where life approaches abysses." This "*deviation from nature* is ... the most agreeable repast for human pride."

It is not speechless affect, but the word that gives delight. Art is based on this "lofty, heroic unnaturalness." It salvages the moment of intense, inscrutable speechlessness in the word. *The transformation into words* is redemptive: "At this point nature is *supposed to be* contradicted. ... The Greeks went far, very far in this respect—alarmingly far." For the Greek poets, the aim was not "to overwhelm the spectator with sentiments." Instead, they transform everything into reason and word, retain no "residue of *silence*" in their hands. The "law of beautiful speeches" is addressed to passion, to the sentiments. The masklike but ceremonial stiffness of Greek actors reflects that unnaturalness that transforms passion into word, abyss into ground, darkness into spiritual brightness, the absence of concepts into *sense and meaning*.

A "deviation from nature" may also take the opposite direction, as a thoroughgoing "lack of regard for words." Rossini, Nietzsche affirms, "had everybody sing nothing but la-la-la." In this "la-la-la," in this musical deviation from nature, Nietzsche glimpsed a reason constituted through the liberation of being from work and passion. This "la-la-la," Nietzsche declares, is the essence of opera, even of music itself: "Confronted with the characters in an opera, we are not supposed to take their word for it, but the sound! That is the difference, that is the beautiful *unnaturalness* for whose sake one goes to the opera." "Serious opera," however, Nietzsche reproaches for its lack of courage: "Occasionally picking up a word must help the inattentive listener, but on the whole the situation must explain itself, and the speeches do not matter! That is what all of them think, and hence they have their fun with the words. Perhaps they merely lacked the courage to express fully their ultimate lack of regard for words." For Nietzsche, not even the *recitativo secco* is a verbal structure beholden to interpretation. It rather permits a "rest from melody" which soon provokes a "new desire for *whole* music, for melody." It is melody, not the word, that animates song. Perhaps all entertainment partakes of the beautiful *unnaturalness*, of that miraculous deviation from nature, which delights and redeems.

In "Orpheus in the Underworld," Theodor Adorno remarks critically on best-selling art music titles. There is something almost peremptory in the distinction he draws between art and popular music.[27] Art is heaven. The popular is the underworld: "Many chart-toppers that accepted standards classify as art music are, in terms of character, popular, or at the very least have grown exhausted and banal through countless repetition: what was art can become popular."[28] Everywhere Adorno suspects "pop music in disguise." Everything is "chirping," "jabbering," "hopping about." Consumers expect nothing but "splendor and pomp": "A primitive notion of vibrancy seems to exert a power of suggestion, as if the purchase of a record were thought to grant one the right to something in color." Passion lacks this vibrancy, this splendor and pomp. Its color is ash gray. Art music dresses in mourning.

Even in Tchaikovsky, Adorno discerns elements of popular music. His work represents a "mingling of the genius and the base." He has a rare talent for creating extraordinarily penetrating yet, for that very reason, often quite vulgar characters. The secret of his music's effect must be sought in a deep-seated stratum of infantilism. His music is "nourished by an ungovernable yearning for joy." It is drunk on the "fulfillment denied those who revel in their daydreams of great passion." This is a child's relationship to happiness. True happiness, however, it not there for the taking. It is possible "only in a broken form," as "a memory of what has been lost, a longing for the unattainable." Tchaikovsky's yearning for joy has not discovered this brokenness through music. His imagery is "not sublimated, but crassly fixed." Entertainment "objectively vitiates those who experience it and who subjectively crave it." It is "no more than a substitute for things people are otherwise disallowed." He concludes: "The world of entertainment is the underworld passing itself off as heaven."

Popular music lacks "great passion." Hence its joy is a false *appearance*. Brokenness alone lends truth and authenticity to joy. Consequently, only the painfully broken, people like Beethoven, the *Homo doloris*, have access to true joy. All true art music is *passion music* in the strictest sense. Adorno describes Beethoven's records as the "pièce de résistance" in the midst of "pop music in disguise."

Not only is Tchaikovsky's ungovernable yearning for joy infantile; so is Adorno's defiant *no*, which condenses into passion. His brokenness is simultaneously a hindrance, an inability to live. His *colorblindness* bars him access to anything but gray. The joy that can only be articulated through brokenness is an illusion. *Every* joy is illusory.

It may be that the most beautiful music, which converges on true joy, rings out in this same underworld. Famously, Orpheus's singing frees existence from suffering all at once. Tantalus no longer reaches for the flowing water. Ixion's wheel stands still. The birds stop tearing at the liver of Tityus. The daughters of Danaus let their jugs lie still. And Sisyphus sits quiet atop his stone. *Work* comes to rest. The air is cleared of passion. Perhaps Eurydice's liberation is divine reward for Orpheus's entertainment in the underworld.

ON LUXURY

The superfluous is the precondition of all beauty.
—Friedrich Nietzsche

In Rossini, Richard Wagner sees the ideal type of the "man of luxury." According to his theory of luxury, this defining characteristic of this reprehensible being is estrangement from the natural or inclination toward the unnatural. The man of luxury exploits the flower for its aroma alone, artificially manufacturing "perfume," in order to "carry it wherever he goes, and sprinkle it on himself and his splendid instrument according to his whims."[1] Like perfume, Rossini's "narcotic, intoxicating melody" is unnatural. Estranged from the naturalness of "songs of the people" or "flowers of the people," Rossini's creations are nothing but "artificial growth."[2] He is an "unusually skilled modeler of artificial flowers, which he has shaped from velvet and silk, painted with flashy colors, splashed in the calyx with aromatic substrates until they exude the scent of true flowers."[3] Wagner cites nature or the natural in opposition to "luxurious unnature."[4] The opera public is, Wagner states, an "unnatural outgrowth of the people," a "caterpillar's nest" that "gnaws at the healthy, nourishing leaves of the tree of the people to glean from it the vital force needed to flap through an ephemeral, luxurious existence as a merry, fluttering flock of butterflies."[5] Light music is ephemeral, a fleeting illusion. "Salacious modern opera music" offers an unnecessary entertainment only good for the satisfaction of "wanton cravings."[6] It is based on a longing for "merely intoxicating and delightful enjoyment."

Wagner turns nature into ideology. Hence he fails to recognize that culture as such is based on deviation, on a luxation of the natural, that the flower in the field, beautiful and splendid as it may be, is not yet culture. The flower of the people is not a natural flower. Indeed, the "natural tree of the people" is an oxymoron. Nor is it culture to "force oneself through boughs, branches, and leaves ... in order to delight in the *sight* of flowers."[7] To the contrary, it is the *abstraction* of scent from flower, the *abstraction* from nature of something proper to oneself, that counts as an achievement of culture. Perfume is an oft-discussed example of the luxation of nature, of the aptitude of culture for abstraction. Silk and velvet flowers steeped in perfume exist thanks to the luxating deviation of nature. *As a consequence, they do not wilt.* Luxury is not a failure of spirit, but an *enhancement of its vitality.* Its sumptuous brilliance is the antithesis of death. It postpones death, which is an *event of nature.*

We have already referred to Nietzsche's aphorism against Wagner, which attributes the origin of culture to an emphatic *"deviation from nature."*[8] According to Nietzsche, even the small stage of tragedy represents a luxation of natural life. Greek tragedy makes passion *eloquent,* "mute" as it may be "in nature," *adorns it with* "beautiful speeches." Its masks engender artificiality as well, abstracting cere-

ON LUXURY

monially from the natural expressions of the face. The absence of facial expressions transforms, *verbalizes, spatializes* the *natural* "sentiments" into a *figure*, an *eloquent gesture*. This process of concentration and compression also characterizes the abstraction of perfume from the nat ural flower.

In Rossini the deviation from the natural occurs in the opposite direction. There is a radical renunciation of the word. As we have previously stated, his utter "lack of regard for words" is the basis of absolute melody, the "la-la-la." This presupposes a deviation from natural passion, which merely stammers. Both unnatural plenitude and unnatural emptiness are a luxation of the natural. This "beautiful *unnaturalness*" is likely what drove Hegel to ecstasy when he attended Rossini's opera. It was *absolute entertainment* that led Hegel to believe he was living in utopia. In relation to "beautiful *unnaturalness*, there is *no fundamental difference*" between Rossini, "smiling to himself in the lush lap of luxury" and "shy, retiring, brooding" Beethoven.[9] Both live on a *beautiful illusion*, whose brilliance is invariably due to *luxation*.

Art demands a luxation of necessity. Its intention is not merely to *redirect necessity*. Other directions determine it as well. Nonetheless, and problematically, Wagner associates art with need. Its subject is the people, the "incarnation of all those ... who *experience a common need*."[10] Art is based on this common need, which is at the same time a *basic necessity* possessed in common. All deviations from this need and necessity are luxury and degeneration. The demand of the people is liable to fulfillment because it is, like hunger, a natural demand. It vanishes in its opposite, in "satiety." But no natural demand, no basic need lies at the base of luxury, which depends, instead, on a proliferating "delusion."[11] Luxury does not address the necessary or pressing, but is guided by an unnatural demand, by a "mad, needless need" that can never be sated, in contrast to "real, felt hunger."[12]

Wagner invokes need frequently. For him it represents a remedy, a magic potion that wards off the "devil" of luxury: "Need will abolish the hell of luxury; it will teach the martyred, apathetic spirits confined in its hell the simple, basic needs of purely human physical hunger and thirst; it will offer us as brothers the nourishing bread, the clear sweet water of Nature; as brothers we shall savor them, as brothers we shall become true men. And as brothers, we shall forge the bond of holy necessity, and the kiss that seals this bond will be the *communal artwork of the future*."[13] The "simple, basic need of purely human physical hunger and thirst" is in reality purely animal. Genuine human need is neither basic nor simple. It is a far more unnatural, "needless need." The intensification of pleasure demands *denaturing*, whereas the satisfaction of merely natural imperatives never goes beyond basic necessity. Moreover, satiety lacks the language and eloquence that are the essential requirements of art and culture. And the soul flourishes only in superfluity. "Bread" and "water," however "sweet" they may be, do not give rise to art. Art is the corollary of a surplus that exceeds the necessary. Still, not even Wagner is prepared to renounce sumptuousness. What satisfies the "*necessary* demands of man" is "the sumptuous excess of nature."[14] To what extent, then, can we distinguish the "luxury" of un-nature from nature's "sumptuous excess"?

Why does Wagner explain hunger and thirst in this way? Apparently he is struggling against a mighty inclination to luxury he senses within himself. Nietzsche must have peered deeply into Wagner's soul. In Wagner he sees a man of luxury: "A passionate longing for luxury and splendor in Wagner; precisely from this he was made capable of understanding this drive to its depths, of passing judgment on it."[15] Not a "natural" demand, but rather a "passionate longing for luxury and splendor," a "mad, needless need," which indeed does spring from a "delusion"—it is this Wagner must thank for his art. Without "delusion," without its opulent *images*, there is nothing but basic necessity. Every splendor, every beauty has its origin in the former.

Following his break with Wagner, Nietzsche elevated luxury to something entirely elementary and *natural*: "*Luxury.*—The penchant for luxury is rooted in man's depths: it reveals as superfluous and immoderate the waters where his soul prefers to swim."[16] In times of need or urgency, the human soul cannot flourish. Its element, its *space* is sumptuous splendor. Luxury is a splendor that glows without illuminating and without revealing anything. It is a free, intentionless splendor that shines simply in order to shine. The splendor of luxury dwells on a particular surface that is free from the *illusion of depth*, and thus appears in beautiful groundlessness.

Nietzsche presupposes a fundamental contradiction between luxury and knowledge. Luxury is "humiliating for the man of knowledge," for it "represents a life different from the simple and heroic one." An entirely distinct intention motivates it, an entirely distinct temporality. The man of luxury looks with suspicion on passion and the heroism of knowledge. For him the essential thing is to submit entirely to the presence of joy. Luxury is "superfluity and immoderation for eye and ear," and in it, one "feels at ease."[17] There is no need to posit an existential divide between the man of luxury and the man of knowledge.

Examined closely, luxury is not detrimental to knowledge. Knowledge is predicated on the mental capacity to decipher fine similarities or dissimilarities among things. Kant calls this "acumen." He traces the "*subtleties*" back to this capacity for distinction. In regard to judgment, "*exactitude*" (*cognitio exacta*) enhances acumen. It is also bolsters the wit, being "the *wealth* of the good mind." Interestingly, Kant describes acuteness as "luxury of minds." It is thus not a property of that "common and *healthy* understanding" that is fixated on "needs." Discernment does not evolve out of need. It is instead predicated on a luxation thereof. Neither *contemplatio* nor *theoria* may arise from need or necessity. They, too, are a "kind of luxury of minds." Wit, Kant states, "*flourishes*" like that nature which "appears in her flowers to be at play, whereas in her fruits, she seems rather to be at work." Viewed in this light, not even nature consists of need or necessity. Sumptuous luxation, the extravagance of shapes and colors of flowers, takes priority over "work."

Thinking, too, *flourishes* only on this side of "work." Knowledge is accordingly the fruit of thought in flower. Need and work alone do not bring it forth.

Every splendor of being exists thanks to luxation. The inclination thereto is constitutive of *spirit* itself. Where no deviation occurs, there is only death. Everything congeals into lifelessness. Luxation occurs in a variety of directions. There is splendor in plenitude, but also splendor in emptiness. And even *asceticism* is more than simple resignation and eschewal. Rather, it is a submission to the plenitude of emptiness. Here, luxury and *asceticism* meet: in the *luxury of the void*.

Surprisingly, Adorno, a man of knowledge through and through, bemoans the disappearance of luxury. Indirection, unconstraint, exuberance, or carefree elaboration increasingly yield to the direct and instrumental: "Rampant technology eliminates luxury. ... The express train that in three nights and two days hurtles across the continent is a miracle, but travelling in it has nothing of the faded splendor of the *train bleu*. What made up the voluptuousness of travel, beginning with the goodbye-waving through the open window, the solicitude of amiable accepters of tips, the ceremonial of mealtimes, the constant feeling of receiving favors that take nothing from anyone else, has passed away, together with the elegant people who were wont to promenade along the platforms before the departure, and who will by now be sought in vain even in the foyers of the most prestigious hotels."[18] Luxury, for Adorno, is the expression of unadulterated joy. It is also constitutive of art. Life thence finds fulfillment in neither practicality nor instrumental reason. Instead, true joy springs from excess, exuberance, sumptuousness, the senseless, the luxation of the necessary. The surplus or superfluous is what frees life from all compulsion. The absence of compulsion or care is moreover an element of entertainment, even of *utopia*, and is the substance of "pure amusement." This is a form of luxury, a luxation of work and necessity, that brings it close to art: "Amusement, free of all restraint, would be not only the opposite of art but its complementary extreme."[19]

SATORI

True poetry presents itself as a secular gospel that knows how to free us, through inner serenity, through outward cheer, from the earthly burdens that weigh us down.

—Johann Wolfgang von Goethe

The construct of true or serious art, strictly separated from mere entertainment, arises in concert with a number of dichotomies characterized by internal tension: reason/ mind versus the senses, for example, or transcendence versus immanence.[1] The positing of dichotomies is characteristic of occidental thinking. Far Eastern thinking, on the other hand, is oriented toward complimentary principles. Rather than stiff oppositions, reciprocal dependencies and correspondences preside over being. The dichotomy of mind versus the senses, which grounds the concept of a low art addressed only to the demands of the senses, never developed in the Far East. Nor does Far Eastern culture recognize the idea of artistic autonomy or the conflation of truth and art. No *passion for truth*, which suffers the extant as false, predominates in Far Eastern art, and it proposes no utopian antithesis to the existing world that serves to negate it. Negativity does not animate Far Eastern art. It is primarily concerned with affirmation and entertainment.

The haiku, the Japanese short poem, is understood in the West almost exclusively in relation to Zen Buddhist spirituality.[2] "Haiku is," a famous saying goes, "a kind of Satori."[3] Seen thus, haiku is an expression of inspiration or redemption. Roland Barthes views the haiku as centered on a very particular metaphysics: "the haiku, [which is] articulated around a metaphysics without subject and without god, corresponds to the Buddhist Mu, to the Zen satori."[4] For Barthes, the haiku represents a speechless wager, "attaining to that anterior shore of language ... contiguous to the *matteness* of the adventure."[5] It releases, redeems language from its obligation to meaning.

The winter wind blows.
The cat's eyes
blink.[6]

Haiku is, Barthes writes, "only" (!) a "literary branch" of the spiritual adventure of Zen. Zen is "an enormous praxis destined to halt language, to jam that kind of internal radiophony continually sending in us, even in our sleep ... to empty out, to stupefy, to dry up the soul's incoercible babble."[7]

It clearly eludes Barthes that haiku is not halting language, but rather is in its own way *chatty* and *entertaining*:

A handle
On the moon—
And what a splendid fan.[8]

This morning, how
Icicles chip!—Slobbering
Year of the Cow![9]

In Japan, haiku is rarely seen as part of an earnest, spiritual attempt to bring an end to the babble of the soul. There is little recognition, in the Western reception of haiku, that it is, above all, ludic and entertaining, less withdrawn into the desolation of meaning than radiant with wit and humor.

Haiku literally means "playful verse." It is originally the seventeen-syllable starting verse (*hokku*) of the linked-verse *haikai no renga. Haikai*, in turn, means "comic." The content of linked verse of this kind is witty, humorous, and occasionally prurient. Its primary purpose is to amuse and delight. Its composition is a communal rather than solitary act, undertaken for the purpose of *entertaining*. It does not occur in a solipsistic space. Conviviality, spontaneity, and the rash *cutting word* typical of the linked verse sequence leave no room for poetic inwardness. Entertainment arises from agreeable inspirations or witty transitions. In any case, brevity and spontaneity preclude the exploration of deeper registers. Verse of this kind is a game played in common, a game of language. Haiku are even frequently composed in groups.[10] They are ill suited to the expression of an individual soul's passion. They are, above all, *too brief* for a *passion narrative*.

> One man
> and one fly
> waiting in this huge room.
> —Issa

Passion, or the emphasis on truth, is not a prerequisite for the refinement of aesthetic expressive forms. Nor do play and entertainment necessarily lead to aesthetic flattening or impoverishment. Without a sense of play or entertainment, haiku would never have arisen. Haiku treats neither of the passion of the soul nor of the adventure of eradicating it. Haiku is more an entertaining game than a spiritual or linguistic adventure.

In Japan, poetry is above all a communal, linguistic game, pleasing and entertaining. It is largely free of pathos or of the passion of the soul. Many poems first arose in the context of verse competitions. Poetry is not the reserve of the elite, but has always reached the broader populace. The general diffusion of aesthetic forms of expression has contributed to an aestheticization of the quotidian.[11] Greater levels of entertainment and play do not automatically signify a loss of aesthetic quality. Indeed, disavowal of entertainment or play may even diminish the aesthetic.

Undoubtedly, Confucian morality has also exerted an influence on the art of the Far East. Rarely, however, is it burdened by an ideological layer.[12] It does not generally move in a critical, subversive, or dissident space.[13] The idea of the avant-garde, the negativity of such an idea, is fundamentally foreign to it. With respect to the extant world, Far Eastern art tends to a more affirmative approach than its Western counterpart. Passion is not its defining feature. Such art occasions no *no*, no appeal to the observer to change what exists. As Far Eastern thinking is not based on dichotomous structures (for example, mind versus the senses), the exalted idea of reconciliation does not arise. Art is not opposed to some alienated reality. It does not embody an emphatic *otherness* that would lift it above the

SATORI

false world, a world stricken with alienation. No aesthetic distance raises art to a distinguished sphere of being.

Particularly in the German cultural field, art is rigorously partitioned into dichotomies. The clear distinction between art and entertainment is based, not least of all, on the dichotomy of mind versus the senses. "*Common*," according to Schiller, is everything "that does not speak to the *mind*, all interest of which is addressed exclusively to the senses."[14] Beethoven's stare, "painfully broken, withered from longing—and yet undaunted unto death" embodies the German principle of spirit, of *Geist*, that is, the *passion principle*.[15] Far Eastern art lacks such an "eerie splendor." It is bare of longing and brokenness.

Japanese *ukiyo-e* woodcuts famously exercised a powerful fascination on many European painters of the modern period, enthralling even Paul Cézanne and Vincent van Gogh. Yet *ukiyo-e* is anything but high art. Instead, it is an art of quotidian and customary life. It was deeply embedded in the entertainment industry that flourished in the Edo period. A popular motif in *ukiyo-e* was the pleasure quarter of Edo Yoshiwara with its beauties, jesters, tea houses, Kabuki theaters, and actors plying their trades. *Ukiyo-e* was a part of this pleasure quarter. Its popularity led to mass production. Portraits of actors in particular sold like mad. *Ukiyo-e* painters also produced erotica, at times showing the sex organs grotesquely exaggerated and in extremely sharp detail.[16] *Ukiyo-e* images were often humorous. *Ukiyo-e* was mass culture, intended to entertain.

Far Eastern art does not define itself in opposition to the everyday world. It does not inhabit a special sphere of being, it is not a window onto transcendence, instead it is an art of immanence. *Ukiyo-e* radically affirms the quotidian, transitory world. No longing for depth, truth, or meaning animates it. Its brilliant colors and clear outlines permit no exploration of depth. *Ukiyo-e* allows *surfaces* to blaze. It is an art of brilliant immanence. The observer's gaze lingers on the brightly colored surface, *searching for nothing*. It is never hermeneutic; it never penetrates. The effect of *ukiyo-e*, like haiku, is unambiguous. Nothing seems *concealed*. A peculiar *evidence* predominates in it. The observer looks, unhindered by hermeticism or hermeneutics. The very name *ukiyo-e* suggests its affirmative character. *Ukiyo-e* literally means "images of the floating world."[17] It submits without resistance to the motley spectacle of a transitory world uncontrasted with any counterworld or *counter-time*. *Ukiyo-e* is an art of the *here and now*, worth affirming despite or even because of its transitoriness. At its core, *ukiyo-e* is *ephemeral*. Stress on the *there* is not proper to the Far Eastern or Japanese representational world. Haiku, too, is oriented wholly toward the *here and now*. Nothing points away toward a *there*. Haiku represents nothing prior or concealed. It is *all there*. It has nothing to hide. Nothing withdraws into the depths. Like *ukiyo-e*, haiku lets the *surface* blaze. This is the nature of the *friendliness* of Far Eastern art.

The following remark by Cézanne would prove equally disconcerting to courtly painters, with their strongly decorative tendencies, as to artists of the popular-plebian *ukiyo-e:* "In a few hundred years, it will be utterly useless to live, everything will be flattened."[18] Cézanne closes this conversation with the words: "Life is terrifying! *And then, like a prayer as night falls, I hear him murmur several times:* 'I want to die painting ... to die painting.'"[19] Cézanne's passion is characteristically European. He conceives of art as a "priesthood" that "demands men of purity."[20] Art is passion. It posits suffering as a higher state of being. Far Eastern art lacks this passion and longing. Even Kabuki theater, which is closely related to *ukiyo-e,* affirms the fleeting and transitory nature of life. Kabuki originally signifies "lack of restraint."[21]

In the preface to *Bunte Steine,* Adalbert Stifter writes: "Occasionally, I have even been reproached for portraying only small things, and told that my people are ordinary people. If that is true, then I am now in the position of offering readers something even smaller and less significant, namely a variety of amusements for young hearts. Not even virtue and morals will be preached here in the usual manner; these will instead have to exert their effects through their own nature."[22] Art is, Stifter continues, "something very high and sublime." Artists are "high priests." He does not presume to affirm that his own writings are art. He does not have in mind the portrayal of "something great or small." Stifter locates his own writing outside of "literature": "Even if every spoken word cannot be literature, it can be something different and not entirely lacking in the right to exist. To brighten the hour of sympathetic friends, to offer a greeting to them, known and unknown alike, and to contribute a grain of good to the edifice of eternity has been and will remain the intention of my writing." Stifter's uncommon modesty, which is possibly a tactical evasion, locates him in a literary space where even a simple, everyday "greeting" has its place. Literature offers people a simple "brightened hour." Writing does not occur in a solipsistic space, in the inner chambers of a single soul. Instead, literature is communication (greeting), companionship, play, cheer, and enjoyment. Prior to considerations of "great or small," it exists on the broad field of the *everyday* and the *customary*. *Immanence* is its domain. Lacking any ideological or moral superstructure, Stifter's writings should "only exert their effects through their own nature." Rigid oppositions like serious versus entertaining or mind versus the senses restrict the space of literature. The art of the everyday disengages from art as passion, as priesthood. Where the longing for transcendence is extinguished, immanence retains a peculiar brilliance. It is the *entire* world.

Far Eastern religions also take an affirmative stance toward the extant. Taoism teaches hewing to the *facticity* of the world, to that which *always already* is. Taoist not-doing is a formula for radical affirmation, the antithesis of *doing as passion*. The way submits entirely to the natural course of things. Taoist thinking, Far Eastern thinking, is imbued not with negation of the world or flight from it, but with trust in the world. Affirmative not-doing as the openness to that which *does itself*—resignation before the world, in other words—is opposed to the intentionality of passion.

Ukiyo-e stems originally from the Buddhist representational schema according to which the world is transitory and fleeting as a dream. The Buddhist concept of "nothing" means that nothing is firm in the world, nothing perseveres; everything flows away and elapses. Any attempt to hold onto something or to strive for something unchangeable is in vain. Instead, redemption is overcoming passion and yearning. *Ukiyo-e* celebrates the world despite, even because of, its fleetingness. *Enjoyment implies affirmation.* This form of approval is different from that consent which, in Adorno's cultural critique, permits the continued existence of the false world. As Adorno said: "To be entertained means to be in agreement."[23]

The affirmation of the transitory is characteristic of the Far East. Passion for the eternal or the definitive is foreign to it. The famous Chinese poet Li Po writes:

> ... the floating life is but a dream,
> so how much joy can we have at all?
> The ancients had good reason to hold candles
> and entertain themselves at night ...[24]

Zen Buddhism, a Far Eastern version of Buddhism, is also a religion of radical affirmation, a religion without passion, pathos, or longing. "Every day is a good day" is a plainspoken formula for redemption. Redemption's place is *everydayness*, the everyday *here and now*, the transitory world, for there is no *other* world, no *outside*, no *there*, no transcendence. It is vain to try to break out of the *here and now*. What is the point, then, of passion or longing? They only produce pain. The everydayness of Zen Buddhism is the antithesis of passion.

I fear Subhuti won't be able to escape him;
Even beyond the cosmos all is filled to the brim.
What end will he know to his frantic turmoil
From all sides the pure wind tugs at his clothes.[25]

In contrast with Christianity, which is a religion of expectation and of promise, a religion of the *there* and of the *future*, Zen Buddhism is a religion of the *here and now*. It is enough to tarry in the *here and now*. And asceticism is not a Zen Buddhist ideal. "Eat!"—this is a famous dictum of the Zen master Yunmen.[26] A redemption aphorism of the Zen Master Linji declares: "When hungry, eat your rice; when tired, close your eyes. Fools may laugh at me, but wise men will know what I mean."[27] Emphatic day-to-day existence precludes *being as passion*. For Zen Buddhism, redemption, satori, lies in this turn toward the everyday, this *deviation* from every form of passion toward the everyday world. As contentment and the absence of longing, as absolute immanence, satori, often expressed as loud laughter, is akin to pure amusement. It laughs away every form of passion: "One evening Yao-shan climbed the mountain for a walk. Seeing the moon suddenly appearing from behind the clouds, he laughed most heartily. The laugh echoed ninety li east of Li-yang where his monastery was."[28]

MORAL ENTERTAINMENT

There is nothing beautiful that does not give
us lasting pleasure, and nothing can give us lasting pleasure,
and the lasting feeling of such, except truth, reason,
and moral order.
—*Der Greis*

For Kant, moral enjoyment or moral pleasure is a contradiction, because morality is duty. Morality is based on a "necessitation," on "intellectual constraint."[1] It expressly rejects the "inclinations," which are the source of enjoyment. Practical reason must overcome the "impetuous importunity of inclinations."[2] This "moral necessitation" results in pain: "Hence we can see a priori that the moral law, as the determining ground of the will, must by thwarting all our inclinations produce a feeling that can be called pain."[3] Morality is passion. Morality is pain. The way to moral perfection, to "saintliness," is a *via doloris*.

Kant's emphasis on reason is undoubtedly rooted in the Enlightenment. And yet, the antagonism to the senses and desire that dominate his theory of morality and his thinking as a whole are not characteristic of the Enlightenment. The Enlightenment was more characterized by a rehabilitation of the sensuous. The Enlightenment is more than Kant; it is also Julien Offray de La Mettrie and his radical affirmation of sensuality and pleasure. The feeling of being, according to La Mettrie, is primarily one of desire and happiness. Kant's hostility to the senses is not a genuine expression of the Enlightenment, but a residuum of Christian morals. Further, his "impetuous importunity of inclinations" is anything but "natural." Only the *sharp cut* that rigorously cleaves reason from the senses produces compulsion, causes injury, permits the inclinations to become "impetuous" and "importuning."

For Kant, the "highest good" is "an a priori necessary object of our will."[4] The "highest good" alone is satisfactory for "the perfect volition of a rational being."[5] But virtue is not the only constituent of the "highest good." Virtue *and* happiness together compose the "complete good." And yet, they are "quite *different elements*" that stand in opposition to one another.[6] Morality as such does not produce happiness. Nor is it a "doctrine of how we are to make ourselves happy," for happiness is a matter of inclinations and sensuousness. Likewise, inclination as a source of happiness does not conduce to moral action, "for human nature does not of its own proper motion accord with the good, but only by virtue of the dominion which reason exercises over sensibility."[7] Domination and pain are therefore necessary for moral progress.

For Kant, a deep gulf separates morality and happiness. Still, he does not care to relinquish happiness for the sake of morals. Kant is always *squinting* in the direction of happiness. In doing so, he is calling on God. God has taken care that "happiness [be] distributed in exact proportion to morality."[8] For the "sacrifice" offered, for the pain suffered, *Homo doloris* receives a "rich compensation."[9] Kant capitalizes on pain for happiness. Passion does not reduce happiness, but augments it. It is a *formula for intensification*, which mortgages happiness for bliss.

The German translation of La Mettrie's *Discours sur le Bonheur*, which he had composed during his Prussian exile, appeared in 1751. Significantly, the title was *The Highest Good, or The Philosophical Thoughts of Monsieur de La Mettrie on Bliss.* Kant was surely familiar with this treatise. Nonetheless, La Mettrie describes his "highest good" in terms very different from Kant's. La Mettrie denies the existence of a contradiction between happiness and virtue that would make recourse to God necessary. Virtue does not represent an absolute grandeur lying beyond all bliss and accessible only through God. Instead, for La Mettrie, morality leads to happiness. Moral enjoyment is not an oxymoron. The happy life is the one that knows how to wrest the possibility of happiness from virtue. This, for La Mettrie, is the very art of living: "People are happier in proportion to the [virtue] they possess ... whereas those who neglect [virtue] and know nothing of the pleasure of practicing it are unsuited to this sort of happiness."[10] La Mettrie repeatedly stresses that there is no contradiction between happiness and morality: "Busy with filling the narrow circle of life, people find themselves all the happier by living not for themselves, but ... for humanity in general, in service to which one attains to glory. With our own happiness, we add to the happiness of society."[11]

Happiness is not the condition of an isolated individual "in the whole of whose existence everything goes according to his wish and will."[12] This Kantian image of happiness is infantile. Happiness does not simply mean that everything occurs as I wish. Happiness has a far more complex, mediated structure extending beyond the immediateness of instantaneous wish fulfillment. Nor is happiness a sensory phenomenon. It is instead the product of social, intersubjective mediation. Thus the moral weekly circular *Der Glückselige* affirms: "Living in a world inhabited by our equals, firmly united with our neighbors, we require others for our happiness, and must in turn labor with helping hands to make others happy. And so we have made a beginning of fellowship, and in *fellowship counseled* happiness with and alongside one another."[13]

Moral weekly papers, a common genre in the eighteenth century, show a different, considerably more human face of the Enlightenment, with no overt hostility to the senses or to pleasure.[14] Not even science or art necessarily exclude entertainment. The "youth" in one is confronted with the motto: "Our science is joy / and art is our pleasure."[15] Already in its first article, the *Patriot* (1724–1726) states: "The path of virtue is not so harsh and austere as many believe. I will attempt to guide my readers through it not in a dour, but in an agreeable way, and hope by doing so to bring them esteem, wealth, and happy days."[16] The path to virtue is no *via doloris*. Morality is not pain and passion. It is not a suspension of joy in life. Instead, moral order promises enduring pleasure. In the *Bürger*, we read: "Self-love will teach him / to be a faithful and obedient subject, a fair and loving townsman / a just and respectful man, a duteous and sober landlord / a sincere and devoted friend / a congenial and polite companion / in brief, to strive to be a useful branch on the trunk of the commonwealth; nor should he forgo his ease and happiness / or yet / yearn to withdraw like an outcast / from the love that grants him life."[17]

The purpose of the moral weeklies extends to offering moral *entertainment for their readers*. For this reason, their contents are light, playful, easy, friendly, joking, representing a kind of literary-moral rococo. Their narratives, which provide a sweet coating for the inherently bitter moral contents, are not their only entertaining aspect. No: joy and pleasure proceed from the moral order itself. The bitter moral core that narrative sugarcoating makes appetizing is insufficient for morality's complex structure of mediation. Morality can, indeed must, be *sweet on its own*. At the very least, it must be pleasing. The reader must be convinced that morality is not necessarily bitter, that it may be reconciled with the "inclinations." Even the *Struwwelpeter*'s success is indicative of the ways moral order can stimulate positive feeling: "How does it come to be that texts which, in the first instance, promote the suppression of the drives, and promise draconian punishments for breaches of their repressive decrees, were read not only with approbation, but apparently with pleasure ...? Is the answer ... that children possess the capacity to ignore while reading everything that does not affect them, and in a certain way enjoy the sugarcoating of amusement while overlooking the bitter pill of moral instruction? Or might avowedly moral texts offer their own immediate pleasure? Is the moral pill perhaps not so bitter after all?"[18]

The entertainment value of moralistic literature arises primarily from the dialectical tension of infraction and the restoration of the moral order, from the deviation from and restoration of the law—in a sense, from guilt and atonement or transgression followed by punishment. Beyond mere enjoyment, moral entertainment media fulfill a social function in a subtle but not insignificant way. They stabilize and habituate the moral order, permit it to seep down into the flesh and blood: in other words, to become *inclination*. They occasion an internalization of the moral norm. Niklas Luhmann too sees the purpose of entertainment as re-impregnating that which *is* or which must be: "It seems that knowledge which viewers already have must be referred to copiously. In this respect, entertainment has an amplifying effect in relation to knowledge that is already present. ... What the romantics longed for in vain, a 'new mythology,' is brought about by the entertainment forms of the mass media. Entertainment re-impregnates what one already is; and, as always, here too feats of memory are tied to opportunities for learning."[19]

Kant's moral theory is more complex than is commonly assumed. It does not exclude from the outset the possibility of moral entertainment.[20] His *"doctrine of the method of pure practical reason"* addresses the question of "the way in which one can provide the laws of pure practical reason with access to the human mind and influence on its maxims, that is, the way in which one can make objectively practical reason subjectively practical as well." Kant himself mentions moral conversation in connection with this doctrine of method: "If one attends to the course of conversation in mixed companies consisting not merely of scholars and subtle reasoners but also of business people or women, one notices that their entertainment includes, besides storytelling and jesting, arguing. ... Now, of all arguments there are none that more excite the participation of persons ... than arguments about the *moral* worth of this or that action by which the character of some person is to be made out. Those for whom anything subtle and refined in theoretical questions is dry and irksome soon join in when it is a question of how to make out the moral import of a good or evil action that has been related, and to an extent one does not otherwise expect of them on any object of speculation they are precise, refined, and subtle in thinking out everything that could lessen or even just make suspect the purity of purpose and consequently the degree of virtue in it."[21] To what degree does conversing over moral questions produce enduring pleasure, even more pleasure than jesting? Kant claims that even children derive pleasure in recognizing the moral contents of a narration, that is, in distinguishing moral duty from inclination. They already possess an "inclination to reason" that leads them "to enter with pleasure upon even the most subtle examination of the practical questions put to them."[22] Kant's moral children "compete with one another" in the "game of judgment." They are "interested" because they sense "progress in their faculty of judgment."[23]

Entertainment that centers on practical questions, to fulfill a moral purpose, must impend on the plane not of feelings but of concepts: "It is altogether contrapurposive to set before children, as a model, actions as noble, magnanimous, meritorious, thinking that one can captivate them by inspiring enthusiasm for such actions."[24] They should be spared "examples of so-called noble (supermeritorious) actions, with which our sentimental writings so abound."[25] In moral terms, the "heroes of romance" also have little effect. What must be offered is "duty ... and the immediate worth that compliance with it gives a person in his own eyes." Morality is passion. It consists of abandoning "the element to which [one] is naturally accustomed ... often not without self-denial," and going "to a higher element in which [one] can maintain [oneself] only with effort and with unceasing apprehension of relapsing."[26]

For Kant, moral entertainment is thus conceivable at most as a "*game* of judgment." People "entertain themselves" gladly through the adjudication of moral examples. These, however, produce no "interest in actions and in their morality itself."[27] Play that involves moral questions is based on disinterestedness. It is an *aesthetic* occupation largely indifferent to the "existence of the object"—in other words, to the *realization* of morality. This is why, beyond engaging the faculty of judgment, moral education requires a "*second* exercise" of drawing "attention, in the lively presentation of the moral disposition in examples, to the purity of will, first only as a negative perfection of the will insofar as in an action from duty no incentives of inclination have any influence on it as determining grounds."[28]

Moral stories, as myths of the everyday that impregnate action with a reassuring *it is so* while also being *entertaining*, may well be more effective in modulating social possibilities than moral "principles" based on "concepts" or the "dry and earnest representation of duty."[29] *Stories* do not argue. They attempt to *please* and *rouse*. This is the basis of their unusual effectiveness. The narrative forms of entertainment proper to mass media contribute to the stabilization of society by habituating moral norms and thereby binding them to the inclinations, to the quotidian, and to the self-evidence of the *it is so*, which requires no supplemental judgment or reflection. Inclinations, which Kant disparages, are in actuality an important building block of the social. It is on them that the social *habitus* depends. The dichotomies Kant clings to, of sensuousness versus reason or inclination versus duty, are abstractions blinding him to essential mechanisms of society and morality.

Kant sees habituation to moral laws as necessary, but he confines it to the plane of *appraisal* and *reflection*. He defines it as "making appraisal of actions by moral laws a natural occupation and, as it were, a habit accompanying all our own free actions as well as our observation of those of others."[30] But feelings or inclinations are not so unstable or unreliable as Kant would have us believe. A moral habitus, a moral automatism of habit, which would take effect *prereflexively*, promises better results than *conscious* decision.

Kant could have taken a phrase from Heinrich Hoffmann, the author of the *Struwwelpeter*, to heart. Heinrich Hoffmann had a quite different vision of moral education and the human soul. It is perhaps no coincidence that he was a doctor in an insane asylum. His doctrine of method states: "With the absolute truth, with algebraic or geometric sentences one moves ... a child's soul not at all, but rather leaves it to atrophy miserably ... and *the* person is happy who knows how to keep alive something of the sense of childhood in his twilight years." Perhaps not only children, but everyone harbors a "sense of childhood," a "child's soul" that responds less to basic principles or dry, earnest notions of duty than to *stories* that entertain, calm, and gratify. Norms become inclinations when presented to the child's soul in the form of a *rhyming* tale. Entertainment is narration. It possesses a narrative *suspense*. A method that generates *suspense* and enmeshes the subject in tension, in thrills, is more effective than compulsion or duty. This is the essence of *myth*, which impends upon the present, its everydayness. The narrativity of myth is likewise a determining factor in entertainment, which is more effective than moral imperatives and more compelling than reason and truth.

HEALTHY ENTERTAINMENT

And so what our elders described in two
golden words as the deepest essence
of all life's rules remains eternally true: pray and work—
God will take care of the rest.

—Christoph Wilhelm Hufeland, *The Art of Prolonging Human Life*

Avoid all sloth,
Which makes time grow longer,
Gives your soul a loathsome tone
And is the workshop of the devil.

—Christoph Wilhelm Hufeland, composed on his deathbed

In the *Critique of Judgment*, Kant cites Voltaire as saying: "heaven has given us two things to compensate us for the many miseries of life, *hope* and *sleep*."[1] Kant would like to see a third, namely laughter, added to these two. He might just as well have said: *good entertainment*, for Kant reflects on laughter and its positive effects in the section dealing with play and entertainment.

Kant counts "games of chance," "harmony," and "wit" as entertainment media.[2] This leads him, problematically, to assign them to the domain of "mere sensations." The pleasure they produce is an "animal, i.e. bodily sensation."[3] Entertainment has no access to knowledge. It gives pleasure, but does not broaden the understanding.

Entertainment occurs on a lower plane than judgments of taste. Its objects are *neither beautiful nor ugly*. They are simply "agreeable." Entertainment appeals immediately to the senses, while the apprehension of the beautiful is a product of reflection, a "judgment."[4] The beautiful is not an object of sensory experience. It is a matter for knowledge and judgment. The beautiful may produce no positive knowledge, but it permits the subject to feel a "harmonization" of its cognitive possibilities. The harmonic play of imagination and understanding, of multiplicity and unity, of sensory and conceptual, is constitutive both of cognition and of the beautiful. In the end, pleasure taken in the beautiful is a *pleasure* the subject takes *in itself*, in its *purposiveness* with regard to knowledge or in its *capacity* for knowledge or cognitive possibilities.

"Agreeable art" is low art or, in modern terms, entertainment. It pleases and entertains by appealing immediately to the senses. It is an object of enjoyment: "Agreeable arts are those which have mere enjoyment for their object. Such are all the charms that can gratify a dinner party." Agreeable art is merely an "entertainment of the moment."[5] It offers no food for thought.

Kant draws a line between agreeable art and fine art, with the latter being synonymous with high art. Fine art is addressed to knowledge, but, as "aesthetic art," it has "the feeling of pleasure [of] what it has immediately in view" in opposition to "mechanical art," whose sole concern is the positive representation of knowledge. In any case, the motive of fine art is not the "pleasure of enjoyment," but

HEALTHY ENTERTAINMENT

rather the pleasure of "reflection" or of gratification subsequent to a distanced *judgment* on the object.[6] "Agreeable art," on the other hand, is governed by enjoyment. It lacks the contemplative calm and distance that would make judgment possible: "and where agreeableness is of the liveliest type, a judgment on the character of the object is so entirely out of place that those who are always intent only on enjoyment (for that is the word used to denote intensity of gratification) would gladly dispense with all judgment."[7]

Kant likewise denies any cognitive dimension to the delight produced by laughter. Understanding, Kant writes, can take no delight in the "absurdity ... present in whatever is to raise a hearty convulsive laugh."[8] The *"strained expectation being suddenly reduced to nothing"* that provokes laughter does not give pleasure to the understanding. "Disappointment" gives no gratification. Problematically, Kant suspects that the origin of gratification lies in the body. Wit may be a "play of thought," but the gratification it offers arises not through thought, but through purely corporeal mechanisms. Kant's theory recalls that strange notion of Descartes's of the pineal gland that binds the soul to the body. Kant proceeds from the assumption that "some movement in the bodily organs is associated sympathetically with all our thoughts."[9] The unforeseen leaps of thought or deviations from the customary constitutive of wit set the body's organs in *"oscillation,"* which "favors the restoration of the equilibrium of the latter, and exerts a beneficial influence upon the health."[10] Gratification is based not on "harmony in tones or flashes of wit," but on harmonic interaction among the body's organs. Gratification is not the "play of representations," but the "play of sensations," the "affect stirring the viscera and the diaphragm."[11] A feeling of bodily well-being emerges from the "reciprocal straining and slackening of the elastic parts of our viscera, which communicates itself to the diaphragm ... in the course of which the lungs expel the air with rapidly succeeding interruptions, resulting in a movement beneficial to health."[12] The nature of the gratification entertainment produces is not mental, but animal, even corporeal-muscular. For Kant, "the feeling of health, arising from a movement of the viscera answering to that play, makes up that entire gratification of an animated gathering upon the spirit and refinement of which we set such store."[13]

Entertainment is healthy because it "agitates the body ... with wholesome motion."[14] The shift between negative and positive sensations produces an "internal motion" that promotes "the whole vital function of the body." Good entertainment is healthy in the manner of an oriental massage: "The agreeable lassitude that follows upon being stirred up in that way by the play of the affects, is a fruition of the state of well-being arising from the restoration of the equilibrium of the various vital forces within us. This, in the last resort, comes to no more than what the Eastern voluptuaries find so soothing when they get their bodies massaged, and all their muscles and joints softly pressed and bent."[15]

Kant denies any cognitive potential to entertainment. It is a sensory-affective event cut off from thinking. Kant fails to notice that beyond being restorative for the body, entertainment is *healthy* in a totally different way: entertainment stabilizes existing social relations. In images and stories, it codifies what *is* and *must be*. It thereby favors the internalization of norms. It does so thanks to its semantic and cognitive structure. Entertainment's effectiveness lies in its ability to infiltrate the cognitive layer beneath the pretext of entertainment and amusement.

Laughter is more than a harmonic play of the viscera and diaphragm that produces a feeling of bodily health. Laughter, incited by a deviation from norms, actually restores and reinforces them. When deviations provoke laughter, norms are reconfirmed. Laughter at others inevitably signifies a reconfirmation of the self, of the trusted and familiar. Hence entertainment does inhabit the cognitive or reflective plane. Gratifying laughter involves not only the diaphragm and the viscera, but also interpretation, judgment. Kant's own chosen example of a joke shows how laughter, contrary to his assumptions, represents an event of the mind. Laughter at the strange invariably implies a feeling of superiority.[16]

Joy based on the beautiful is found in "*restful* contemplation."[17] Contemplative restfulness renders the beautiful inappropriate for entertainment, which is based on "motion." The mind is swayed through sensation. It is "aroused" in the face of the sublime.[18] But the sublime is no more entertaining than the beautiful, because it is not an "animal, i.e. bodily sensation." Instead, it approximates transcendence.

The sublime, for Kant, is that which eludes sensory representation. For the imagination, the sublime is "an abyss in which it fears to lose itself."[19] The sublime does not *solidify* into an *image*. Its negativity provokes fear and reluctance. Yet it exercises a positive effect on the imagination, which is encouraged to abandon the sensory for the transcendental. This crossing over to the transcendental is accompanied by pleasure, a feeling of the "the supremacy of our cognitive faculties on the rational side over the greatest faculty of sensibility." Confronted with the sublime, the subject feels itself raised above the sensory. Sublimity is thus a subjective feeling of *elevation over* the sensory projected erroneously by the subject onto an object.

Sublimity is a contradictory feeling of reluctance and pleasure generated by the "rapidly alternating repulsion and attraction" of the object. This *tension*, this motion generated by the sublime, does not produce entertainment, because the feeling of the sublime is always bound to transcendence, to *ideas*. It disposition is transcendent, or it is attuned to transcendence, while the gratification that arises from entertainment remains a sensory or affective phenomenon, one of animal-bodily impressions. Violent movements of the mind, provoked by the rapid alternation of positive and negative sentiments, do produce gratification insofar as they agitate and stimulate the mind. But without spurring the mind to transcendence, they cannot invoke the feeling of sublimity: "even impetuous movements of the mind ... no matter how much they strain the imagination, can in no way lay claim to the honor of a *sublime* presentation, if they do not leave behind them a temper of mind which, though it be only indirectly, has an influence upon the consciousness of the mind's strength and resoluteness in respect of that which carries with it pure intellectual purposiveness (the supersensible). For, in the absence of this, all these emotions belong only to *motion*, which we welcome in the interests of good health."[20]

We seek out sensory agitation solely for the sake of healthy entertainment, which at the same time gives the mind a healthy jolt. But so long as this motion remains sensory-affective, it is no more than a gratifying *thrill* incapable of invoking any sense of the sublime. As a thrill, a kick, it fails to "expand" the soul.[21] It lacks all transcendence, any relation to the supersensory, any *passion*. It is animal, even brutish gratification.

Kant is no believer in Schilller's famous phrase: "Man is only wholly man when he is at play." At best, the person who gives himself over to play and entertainment is for Kant "wholly man" because he is *also an animal*. The gratification proceeding from play and entertainment is an animal sensation with its source in the viscera, the diaphragm, and the lungs. Entertainment resembles massage in that nothing is "learned" or "thought" in the course of it.[22] The rapid alternation of positive (i.e., hope) and negative (i.e., fear) sentiments enlivens only the vital function of the body. Eastern massage is not entertainment because its principle of alternation is "entirely external," while entertainment is based on an *internal* sensory motion. Yet the end effects, the feelings of health produced by entertainment and massage are not fundamentally different. The feeling of well-being induced by entertainment media is *wellness*. Nothing is "thought" or "learned." The body is simply "agitated ... with wholesome motion."

Interestingly, Kant, in the chapter on play and entertainment, speaks often of health. Entertainment makes one healthy. Laughter produces "an equilibrium of the vital forces of the body."[23] This promotes "bodily well-being," the phrase used in an English translation of 1892.[24] Today one would simply call this "wellness." Entertainment corresponds to a "feeling of health," "well-being," and "wellness."

Undoubtedly, Kant has the Enlightenment to thank for his interest in health. But for him, health is not a purely positive value or final telos. Instead, Kant subordinates it to the teleology of reason: "To all that possess it, [health] is immediately agreeable—at least negatively, i.e. as absence of all bodily pains. But, if we are to say that it is good, we must further apply to reason to direct it to ends, that is, we must regard it as a state that puts us in a congenial mood for all we have to do."[25] Entertainment may promote the "whole vital function of the body." But this whole vital function as such lacks, so to speak, an idea of what it has to do.[26] It serves nothing but bare life. Only reason can join health to an end, conditioning it through a "thing to be done." Kant calls into question the presumption that "there is any intrinsic worth in the existence of one who merely lives for *enjoyment*, however busy he may be in this respect." Absolute worth only characterizes the person who does what he does "heedless of enjoyment." *Doing as passion* determines human existence. "Bodily well-being" is a merely animal sensation. Gratification does not raise humankind above the condition of animals.

But Kant does not relinquish happiness and gratification. His desire, the desire of reason, is for absolute happiness, absolute gratification. Kant mortgages happiness for the "highest good," which contains within itself bliss, a superlative form of happiness. Kant *speculates* with happiness.

In the depths of his soul, Kant is perhaps a *Homo delectionis*. He dons the straitjacket of reason to master his longing for pleasure or his immoderate powers of imagination. The constraints Kant submits himself to produce pain. The internalization of pain makes him a *Homo doloris*. At the same time, it makes pain a source of pleasure. In this way, pain is transformed into passion. It even *intensifies* pleasure.

In Kant's *Anthropology*, pain is raised to a life-principle. Only thanks to pain do we feel alive: "To feel one's life, to enjoy oneself, is thus nothing more than to feel oneself continuously driven to leave the present state (which must therefore be a pain that recurs just as often as the present)."[27] "*Contentment* (acquiescentia)" is beyond our grasp. "As an incentive to activity, nature has put pain in the human being that he cannot escape from."[28] Pain holds deadly lifelessness at bay: "to be (absolutely) contented in life would be idle *rest* and the standstill of all incentives, or the dulling of sensations and the activity connected with them. However, such a state is no more compatible with the intellectual life of the human being than the stopping of the heart in an animal's body, where death follows inevitably unless a new stimulus (through pain) is sent."[29] Work is thus "the best way of enjoying one's life," because "it is an arduous occupation (disagreeable in itself and pleasing only through success)."[30] Pain spurs us "always to progress toward what is better." The path to betterment is a *via doloris*. Pain is healthy. It postpones death.

The Enlightenment is health conscious. Religion is healthy. Morality is also healthy. Thus Kant speaks of "ethical gymnastics."[31] Virtue is an aid to *wellness.* "The power of reason" frees the mind from "pathological feelings" and inclinations and sensations of a pathological bent.[32] In *The Conflict of the Faculties*, Kant describes "moral-practical philosophy" as a "panacea" which, "though it is certainly not the complete answer to every problem, must be an ingredient in every prescription." Kant ascribes to it the capacity "of *preventing* illness" and "of prolonging human life." Beyond the "mere diet" or "gymnastics" of practical reason, philosophy must be a "pharmaceutical (material medica)."[33] Through the "immediate *physical effect* of philosophy, nature carries out its intention (physical health)" and even "overpowers" a "serious attack of gout."[34] Reason makes one healthy. Reason is thus, in relation to health, not at all antithetical to entertainment. Both are healthy. Health is a convergence point where reason and entertainment meet.

BEING AS PASSION

Gesthemane hours of my life
In the dull glow
Of glum apprehension
You have often seen me.
Crying I shout: never in vain.
My young being
Weary of plaints
Trusted none but the angel of mercy.

—Martin Heidegger

In an essay on entertainment, Peter Glotz hints at a possible connection between the critique of entertainment and the passion for death: "The condemnation of entertainment, diversion, light art, has religious roots. In Pascal, for example, for whom 'diversion' disrupted concentration on a life centered around death."[1] Martin Heidegger, too, stands in this intellectual, even theological tradition, which perceives in entertainment a lapse, even apostasy, from the authentic form of life. Distraction is, for Heidegger, a "flight from death."[2] It circumvents the "possibility of *authentic existence*" for Dasein.[3] Only by facing death as "the measureless impossibility of existence" does Dasein become aware of the possibility of authentic existence.[4] As on many other occasions, Heidegger resorts here to the language of the

Christian religion. Dasein is exposed to the "constant temptation of falling-prey." Being-in-the-world is *tempting*."[5] Diversion leads to "falling-prey." It is the antagonist of an earnest, struggling life centered on death.[6] "Struggle" and resoluteness are essential to Heidegger's existential-ontological vocabulary.[7] In "struggling" resoluteness, Dasein "chooses its heroes," according to Heidegger. *Existence is passion*. It is even a passion unto death.

The term "entertainment" does not belong to the vocabulary of *Being and Time*. But Heidegger's existential-ontological analysis of "everydayness" contains the lineaments of a potential phenomenology of entertainment. Heidegger's "they" may be interpreted as the subject of mass entertainment, even as the hypersubject of mass media: "In utilizing public transportation, in the use of information services such as the newspaper, every other is like the next. This being with-one-another dissolves one's own Dasein completely into the kind of being of 'the others' in such a way that the others, as distinguishable and explicit, disappear more and more. In this inconspicuousness and unascertainability, the they unfolds its true dictatorship. We enjoy ourselves and have fun the way *they* enjoy themselves. We read, see, and judge literature and the way *they* see and judge."[8] The they embodies, even verbalizes the horizon of average meaning and understanding according to which the masses understand *themselves* and the world. The they comprises everyday patterns of understanding and conduct to which the masses are oriented. The they is constitutive for understanding, for its patterns of apprehension generate a reality, an "everyday and stubborn reality."[9]

In numerous ways, entertainment media impart patterns of interpretation and conduct. Entertainment thus *maintains* the world. Entertaining is also *maintaining*. Television, which is never addressed in *Being and Time*, may be considered a defining medium for the they. It does not passively display an "objective" reality. Instead it actively produces reality, or that which must be taken as real. Television is a *reality machine*. Watching television (fernsehen) does not produce *distance* (Ferne), instead it engenders *proximity*. It places distance at a distance by configuring reality as *proximity to "the everyday way of being interpreted."*

Mass entertainment permits meanings and values to circulate on *narrative and emotive* pathways. It also shapes feelings, which are constitutive for apprehension: "The domination of the public way in which things have been interpreted has already decided upon even the possibilities of being attuned, that is, about the basic way in which Dasein lets itself be affected by the world. The they prescribes that attunement, it determines what and how one 'sees.'"[10] The function of entertainment media is to *re-impregnate* the "public way in which things have been interpreted" which is determined by "average understanding" or the *normal* view of the world.[11] Conduct and interpretation patterns are internalized through physical and psychological *channels of desire*. In this way, entertainment stabilizes the existing social structure. The they is sustained insofar as the they is entertained. The meaning-structure, which may only be *reproduced*, "*disburdens*" judgment and understanding.[12] The *invention of a world*, of something *completely alien* is far more laborious and demanding than the discovery of an already *interpreted* world. Television too effects a "dis-burdening of being" by proffering prefabricated meaning-formations or *myths*: "And since the they constantly accommodates Dasein, it retains and entrenches its stubborn dominance."[13] Hence, entertainment is not the antithesis of "care," is not a *careless giving-oneself-over to the world*, but is rather a depraved form of "care" in which Dasein is *concerned* with things that un-*burden* its existence.

Entertainment is an *unburdening of being* that generates *pleasure*. This is the conclusion of a phenomenology of entertainment based on Heidegger's analysis of everydayness. "Idle talk" unburdens *talk*. It represents the sum or whole of everyday meaning-formations or convictions: "The groundlessness of idle talk is no obstacle to its being public, but encourages it. Idle talk is the possibility of understanding everything without any previous appropriation of the matter."[14] Gossip and scandal are also "idle talk." As forms of entertainment, they help preserve "the public way of being interpreted." They do not celebrate meaninglessness, but instead possess their own form of *disclosedness*. Everydayness is rife with average presentations of meaning that people consent to unawares: "This interpretedness of idle talk has always already settled itself down in Dasein. We get to know many things initially in this way, and some things never get beyond such an average understanding. Dasein can never escape the everyday way of being interpreted into which Dasein has grown initially."[15]

Heidegger does not consistently describe the they or idle talk in phenomenologically neutral terms. Frequently his interpretation is colored by value judgments or representations with clearly religious roots. Idle talk retains a "disparaging sense." Heidegger's value judgments let what is positive in everydayness slips continually into the negativity of the inauthentic. Everydayness talks into the ground any possibility of authentic existence: "Ontologically, this means that when Dasein maintains itself in idle talk, it is-as being-in-the-world-cut off from the primary and primordially genuine relations of being toward the world, toward Mitdasein, toward being-in itself."[16] Idle talk is contrasted with its positively inflected counterpart, the *passionate form of talk* that is "*keeping silent*," which renders audible the "uncanniness of the suspension." The they un-*burdens* existence. But being as such is *burdensome*. Being is passion. The they and entertainment dis*passion* existence into "the groundlessness and nothingness of inauthentic everydayness."[17] In truth, idle talk is everything but groundless: it establishes or reinforces a *communicative ground*. Groundless or cryptic would better describe that keeping-silent which congeals into passion.

Being and Time could equally have been called *Passion and Entertainment*. *Homo doloris* as a passion figure represents the antithesis of the they. Only in the "primordial individuation of reticent resoluteness that expects *Angst* of itself" does Dasein arrive at authentic existence.[18] Passion is individuation. *Homo doloris* is also *Homo solitudinis*. Entertainment is different: it gives no impression of individuality. In contrast to the they, which sustains the familiar and "holds any new questioning and discussion at a distance because it presumes it has understood and in a peculiar way it suppresses them and holds them back," Heidegger's *Homo solitudinis* ventures forward into the *uncertain*.[19] He exposes himself to that angst which frees him from "the illusions of the they."[20] "Thus Angst takes away from Dasein the possibility of understanding itself, falling prey, in terms of the 'world' and the public way of being interpreted."[21]

Acquiescence to the world is constitutive of falling-prey. Entertainment too is based on acquiescence to what *is*. It is condemned to *generate* or at the very least sustain what is. Angst as the reagent of authentic existence is a *negative* expression in this respect. It comprises "clinging to whatever existence one has reached."[22] It leaves Dasein *homeless* by tearing Dasein away from the familiar world. Entertainment, on the other hand, makes Dasein *at home* in the *present* world. It *maintains the home*. Entertainment is *homekeeping*. In the face of death, Dasein finds itself *away from home*. It becomes aware of that uncanniness of being that remains concealed in the unambiguous, familiar world of the they.

In falling-prey, Dasein's striving does not extend past the known and familiar. Its condition is one of acquiescence to the world. Dasein has *always already arrived*. The "temporality of falling-prey" is the "present."[23] The future is only a pale continuation and extension of the here and now. The temporality of falling-prey excludes the *completely other*. For it, the *future* in the emphatic sense, in the sense of the *recognized-as-approaching*, is closed. The temporality of falling-prey is also that of entertainment. The Dasein that entertains itself clings to the here and now. Entertainment reinforces that which *is*. Its temporality is also the present. The past is the old. The new is what is to come. But neither the old nor the new are the *other*.

The passion of authentic existence exhibits an entirely different time structure. In contrast to falling-prey, what determines it is not the present but the future. The future is the temporality of passion. A messianic future, in which the *completely other* discloses itself, may well by foreign to Heidegger's thinking, but his authentic future as "anticipation of death" does abandon the known and familiar. It makes the world appear in light of "not-being-at-home," casting Dasein out of the "being-at-home of publicness."[24] "Not-being-at-home" drives Dasein to *passion*, compels it to heroic resolution.

The *passion* of authenticity presides over Heidegger's *Being and Time*. The they remains a form of degeneration. Despite his protestations to the contrary, Heidegger's approach to it is not ontologically neutral. It forces into the background the constitutive function of unimpassioned everydayness, of the they, which among other things consists of tending to the world through patterns of meaning and identification, *maintaining* it in a special sense.

Heidegger's Dasein primarily and above all resides in the "work world." Already in *Being and Time*, Heidegger grasps *work* as a basic form of human existence. The *first world* is the "work world." *Work* is guided by "circumspection." Circumspection discovers things in their *whereto*, that is, in their *meaning*, and reflexively, prior to any expressive thematization. It creates a *nearness* to things by classifying them in or *admitting* them into the functional context of the familiar work world. They are *situated* within the work world in accordance with their particular *whereto*. Heidegger calls this admitting, situating bringing-into-nearness of things "de-distancing." De-distancing "circumspection" as "nearness" eradicates distance. But if work ceases, then circumspection sheds its association with the work world. This generates free time as time liberated from work, wherein "circumspection becomes free." Possessed of an *"essential tendency toward nearness,"* Dasein perpetuates the activity of de-distancing outside of the work world.[25] In its free time it wanders through "a distant and strange world," appropriating it "only in its *outward appearance,*" *gawking* at it, as Heidegger might say. In free time Dasein *looks* into the *distance.* This looking-into-the-distance has its own particular mode of vision: "Dasein seeks distance solely to bring it near in its outward appearance. Dasein lets itself be intrigued just by the outward appearance of the world."[26] In its free time, Dasein, liberated from circumspection, gives itself over to the "lust of the eyes," its craving for *images.* It *looks into the distance.*[27]

Heidegger's remark on "free circumspection" may also be read as a critique of television: "When curiosity has become free, it takes care to see not order to understand what it sees, that is, to come to a being toward it, but *only* in order to see. It seeks novelty only to leap from it again to another novelty. The care of seeing is not concerned with comprehending and knowingly being in the truth, but the possibilities of abandoning itself to the world. Thus curiosity is characterized by a specific *not-staying* with what is nearest. Consequently, it also does not seek the leisure of reflective staying, but rather restlessness and excitement from continual novelty and changing encounters. In not-staying, curiosity makes sure of the constant possibility of *distraction*." Television viewing, then, is a passive "being delivered over to the world." Only images are consumed. Curious, restive seeing is analogous to channel surfing. Dasein channel surfs through the world. Channel surfing as "not staying" is, translated into ontological terms, an inauthentic mode of being-in-the-world. Channel surfing ontologically disperses Dasein in an inauthentic existence.

In the year *Being and Time* was published (1927), Heidegger was not yet familiar with television. In Germany the first experimental broadcasts took place in 1934. *Being and Time* does, however, expressly address radio, which enables a kind of *distance-hearing*. Heidegger views relates radio to the aforementioned *"essential tendency toward nearness"*: "All kinds of increasing speed which we are more or less compelled to go along with today push for overcoming distance. With the 'radio,' for example, Dasein is bringing about today a de-distancing of the 'world' which is unforeseeable in its meaning for Dasein, by way of expanding and destroying the everyday surrounding world."[28] Heidegger is unusually judgmental here. But his ontology of the Dasein alone fails to clarify why radio simultaneously expands and destroys the "everyday surrounding world," which is destroyed to the very degree to which the de-distancing of the world is adjudged negative. Is the true world, which would mean *home*, destroyed through the sounds or images of the "distant and strange world"? Or do images themselves, as *mere representations*, destroy what is worldly in the world? Some thirty years later, Heidegger expresses himself more clearly with regard to the massive diffusion of television: images and representations merely propagate a world that is in fact no world: "And those who *have* stayed on in their homeland? Often they are still more homeless than those who have been driven from their homeland. Hourly and daily they are chained to radio and television. Week after week the movies carry them off into uncommon, but often merely common, realms of the imagination, and give the illusion of a world that is no world."[29]

The late Heidegger likewise mistrusts the eye and the image. His critique of "representation" is in its way a critique of the image. Images do not only disclose; they also enclose or conceal. They divert vision from *the preeminent*, from *the real*, both of which evade mediated representation. An interesting apercu appears in Heidegger's often-mocked essay "Why Do I Stay in the Provinces?" After a detailed description of his hut in Todtnauberg, he remarks:

> This is my work world—seen with the eye of an observer: the guest or summer vacationer. Strictly speaking I never myself observe the landscape. I experience its hourly changes, day and night, in the great comings and goings of the seasons. The gravity of the mountains and the hardness of the primeval rock, the

slow and deliberate growth of the fir trees, the brilliant, simple splendor of the meadows in bloom, the rush of the mountain brook in the long autumn night, the stern simplicity of the flatlands covered in snow—all of this moves and flows through and penetrates daily existence up there, and not in forced moments of "aesthetic" immersion or artificial empathy, but only when one's own existence stands in its work. It is the work alone that opens up space for the reality that is these mountains. The course of the work remains embedded in what happens in the landscape.[30]

Heidegger speaks critically of "the eye of an observer." World and landscape elude mere *observation*. The *worldly* in the world cannot be objectified as image or representation. The "gravity of the mountains" and the "hardness of the primeval rock" are what is *real* in the world. The world emerges as *resistance,* which work alone can share in. Whoever does not work, whoever merely observes and enjoys like a *tourist,* thus has no access to the world. Emphasis is placed repeatedly on work. Only work grants access to the world. Only work "opens up space" for "the reality that is these mountains." Mere observation leads to the vanishing of the world. The *real* in the world is only accessible prior to *media dissemination*. It reveals itself only in the *moving and flowing through* and *penetrating* of meadows in bloom and flatlands covered in snow, the rush of the mountain brook and the deliberate growth of the fir trees: "all this moves and flows through and penetrates." *Media* destroy this moving and flowing through and penetrating proper to the *real*.

Media replace "daily existence" (this expression, *tägliche Dasein*, still bears echoes of *Being and Time*) with "realms of the imagination, and give the illusion of a world that is no world."

Gravity and *sustenance* compose the *facticity of the world*. Heidegger's objection to media is, in the end, that media images *de-factify* the world, that they cannot sustain the *weight of the world*, the *particular weight of things*. The medial eventuates in the disappearance of the real. Heidegger lays special stress on the characteristics of things that evade media representation or mere seeing, such as "the gravity of the mountains" or "the hardness and scent of oak."[31] Neither the "scent of oak" nor the "deliberate growth of the firs" may be objectified through media. Authentic things, the things of an *integrated* world, have a special gravity, a special *materiality* opposed to *mediality*. The *weightlessness* of the medial, virtual world defactifies the world. Only the "the wide expanse of everything that grows" "bestows world," Heidegger states.[32] Medial things do not grow, but are instead *produced*. Things that *grow*, that are *integrated*, that are *rooted*, are opposed in Heidegger to medially produced, defactified things.

Heidegger's thinking comprises a *refactification* of the world, above all on the linguistic plane. Rhymes and half-rhymes (delight/autumn night, fir/pasture) suggest an original, unspoiled order in the world which eludes both representation and medial fabrication. The refactification of the world is enabled by a refactification of language. This is true for Heidegger's things, as well. Heidegger's things are

BEING AS PASSION

well known: "brook and bluff," "mirror and clasp," "book and picture," "crown and cross."[33] Alliteration binds these things to an originary world. They make up a reality perhaps no less unreal or virtual than the world of medial things.

Heidegger's expressions—"hardness," "gravity," "gloom," "obscurity," or "burden"— not only evoke the facticity of the world; they also propagate his language of passion. *Being is suffering*. During *entertainment*, which un*burdens* Dasein, we distance ourselves from being as passion. Only *work* corresponds to the passional character of being. Heidegger's emphasis on work persists through the transition from the work-world to the mountain-world. In "Why Do I Stay in the Provinces," he states: "It is the work alone that opens up space for the reality that is these mountains. The course of the work remains embedded in what happens in the landscape." Even work is, particularly in the late Heidegger, not a form of *action*, of *making* or *producing*. It is *passion*. It is based on thrownness. In its peculiar passivity and passion it attends to "what happens in the landscape."

For Heidegger, thinking, too, is work. Thinking as work is, again, passion. It is distinguished by the passivity of "suffering." The task of thinking consists in being "an echo." "To be an echo is the suffering of thinking. Its passion is quiet sobriety."[34] Sober passion is an oxymoron. But Heidegger understands passion in the original sense of *passio* or suffering, as passivity in self-sacrifice or self-surrender to the *given* matter of thought, which is accessible not to active grasping but rather to passive suffering. Thinking must allow itself to be determined (*be-stimmen*), modulated (*durch-stimmen*), indeed overruled (*über-stimmen*) by "what cannot be thought in advance" or by "what sustains and binds."[35] This is the basis of the *facticity of thinking*.

Heidegger's thinker is a *man of pain*. His *theology of pain* runs as follows: "In the rift of pain, what is granted on high guards its perseverance. The rift of pain rends the veiled procession of grace into an un-needed arrival of favor."[36] The rift in thinking is an opening for the "magnitude" that is "too great for humans." The closed *inwardness* of thinking without this rift is not receptive to the "arrival of favor." Only the rift, only pain opens human thinking for the *super*human. Pain is transcendence. Pain is god. Entertainment is immanence. It is godlessness. Heidegger's inclination toward passion is mirrored in his selection of things. Notably, his last things are "crown and cross." By its proximity to "cross," "crown" recollects the crown of thorns of *Homo doloris*. Heidegger calls to God in despair when faced with the world of "machinations" defactified by technology and media: "Only a god can save us."[37] *Being* as pain, as *prayer*, is opposed to the *immanence of beings*, which in the modern era is irremediably submitted to experience and entertainment. Entertainment is a kind of machination that dispenses with all "timidity" before the divine, before that which cannot be thought in advance.

In many respects, Peter Handke is in agreement with Heidegger. In Handke, the defactification of the world is "dépaysement," disorientation or "being out of the country."[38] The media world obviates, one could also say, authentic *being-in-the-world*. Heidegger equates "the stern simplicity of the flatlands covered in snow" in the Black Forest in winter with the happiness of *being-in-the-world* as *being-at-work*. For his part, Handke sets forth on a winter journey to the Danube, Sava, Morava, and Drina Rivers. Handke grasps the happiness of "repaysement," or "repatriation," of being-thrown-back-into-the-world, while "pressing the ancient iron door-handle" and "pushing open the shop door almost laboriously." The facticity of the world appears primarily through *gravity*, through the *resistance* of things: "In the mild resistance of things, generated by age and material gravity, in their contact with the body of the person entering, an independent counter-body reveals itself. ... The Serbian shop door is literally an object, part of a momentary intensive communication of bodies, even the subject of a spatial-concrete event, possessed of its own existence. ... This slight resistance, the detectable inner force of the simplest things, draws them away from representation, salvages them from disappearance into the rehearsed accessibility of perception."[39] His true things, however, once brought into language, that is, translated into signs, again resonate with the unreal and the ghastly: "forest-dark honey pots, soup chickens big as turkeys, oddly yellow noodle nests or crowns and the often predator-mouthed, often storybook fat river fish."[40] This *storybook world* is just as unreal as the media world. Its strangely manipulated language generates a kind of virtual world.

Medial things, which whir through space without gravity, which are everywhere, that is to say, nowhere, must also have struck Handke as ghastly. They certainly bothered

Kafka a great deal. Media for him are ghosts that de-realize the world, that divest it of its *grasp*-ability:

> The easy possibility of writing letters—from a purely theoretical point of view—must have brought wrack and ruin to the souls of the world. Writing letters is actually an intercourse with ghosts and by no means just with the ghost of the addressee but also with one's own ghost. ... How did people ever get the idea they could communicate with one another by letter! One can think about someone far away and one can hold on to someone nearby; everything else is beyond human power. ... Written kisses never arrive at their destination; the ghosts drink them up along the way. It is this ample nourishment which enables them to multiply so enormously. People sense this and struggle against it; in order to eliminate as much of the ghosts' power as possible and to attain a natural intercourse, a tranquility of soul, they have invented trains, cars, aeroplanes—but nothing helps anymore: These are evidently inventions devised at the moment of crashing. The opposing side is so much calmer and stronger; after the postal system, the ghosts invented the telegraph, the telephone, the wireless. They will not starve, but we will perish.[41]

Kafka's ghosts have in the meantime invented television, the internet, and email. These are disembodied means of communication, and for this reason are ghastly. "We will perish"—Handke too might have said this with regard to medial things, which whir without bodies or gravity around the entire planet, and render *true witnessing* impossible. Media messages and images are ghosts that procreate independently of human beings: "Writing letters is actually an intercourse with ghosts and by no means just with the ghost of the addressee but also with one's own ghost, which secretly evolves inside the letter one is writing or even in a whole series of letters, where one letter corroborates another and can refer to it as witness."[42] Everything, following Handke, is ghastly reflections unrelated to *reality*: "Nearly all the photographs and reports of the last four years ... seemed to me increasingly to be simple mirrorings of the usual coordinated perspectives—distorted reflections in the very cells of our eyes and not eyewitness accounts."

Media make people blind. They generate a world without witnessing. They do not bear witness to *reality*. They falsify and *de*flect the world. Their "machinations" obscure its facticity. Dasein, on the other hand, is a being-thrown. The human Dasein exists thanks to the "appeal of the highest heaven" and "protection of sustaining earth."[43] One ought to respond to this appeal and let oneself be borne by that which oversteps the human. Neither human Dasein nor the world is *producible*. This is the basis of their facticity. As humans, we are determined and modulated by "what cannot be thought in advance." This is the basis of our facticity. Only so long as our thrownness, our facticity, resides within ourselves are we safe from becoming a "slave" of "machinations." People are, Heidegger states, "servile to their future." Distraction, which in *Being and Time* cuts Dasein off from authentic existence, makes people deaf to the language of the future: "But the call of the pathway speaks only as long as there are men, born in its atmosphere, who can hear it. They are servants of their origin, not slaves of machination. ... The danger looms that men of today cannot hear its language. The only thing they hear is the noise of the media, which they almost always take for the voice of God. So man becomes disoriented and loses his way. To the disoriented, the simple seems monotonous."[44]

"Book" and "mirror" make the language of the future audible. Film and television deafen the ear to it, so that people grow hard of hearing and distracted. The book is bearing witness. Film is a machination. "Jug" and "plow" are traces of origin. They are not "devices." Radio and television, on the other hand, lead to homelessness. Heidegger constructs the *authentic* world through a highly arbitrary distinction. What Heidegger lacks is *serenity before the world*. His language of passion is willful, and achieves its effects through crude selection and exclusion. It is not *friendly*. Not only "herons" and "deer" belong to the world, but also mice and Mickey Mouse.

A HUNGER ARTIST

To find the way to art, to yield to it, I would almost say, demands first of all repeated damage inflicted on the soul.
—Robert Musil

In a letter to Max Brod, Kafka writes: "Writing is a sweet and wonderful reward, but for what? In the night it became clear to me, as clear as a child's lesson book, that it is the reward for serving the devil." Writing is passion. Its precondition is suffering. The writer gets a reward for being "nipped by the devil's pincers, cudgeled, and almost ground to pieces." Kafka does admit there must be "other forms of writing" perhaps "writing one's stories in the sunlight." But he himself only knows this writing "at night, when fear keeps me from sleeping." Thus he lives on "frail ground or rather altogether nonexistent ground ... over a darkness from which the dark power emerges when it wills and, heedless of my stammering, destroys my life." Kafka asks himself if his life would be better if he no longer wrote, if he said no. But life then would be "wholly unbearable" and would have to "end in madness": "the existence of the writer is truly dependent upon his desk and if he wants to keep madness at bay he must never go far from his desk, he must hold on to it with his teeth."[1]

Writing sustains life—but a life that is no longer life, properly speaking: "Writing sustains me, but is it not more accurate to say that it sustains this kind of life?" The life of the writer resembles death. He does not live, he continually dies. He leads a life turned literally toward death: "I have remained clay, I have not blown the spark into fire, but only used it to light up my corpse." The writer "has a terrible fear of dying because he has not yet lived." He cannot simply "move into the house." His angst before death is thus fictive, because he has not yet lived. How can one feel angst toward the end of life when one doesn't even know what life is? Thus Kafka asks: "What right have I to be alarmed when the house suddenly collapses. After all, I know what preceded the collapse. Did I not emigrate and leave the house to all the evil powers?"

The writer leaves the house, and becomes a *peregrinus* in the desert: "The mental desert. The corpses in the caravan of your first and last days."[2] The writer is animated by the wish *to arrive*, to be home, even to *dream up* a home: "I am away from home and must always write home, even if any home of mine has long since floated away into eternity. All this writing is nothing but Robinson Crusoe's flag hoisted at the highest point of the island." Writing is writing toward home, a pilgrimage toward a final home.

Writing is passion. It is a continual rescue attempt that turns into its opposite. The writer rescues himself through his downfall, in the literal sense of the term. Rescue shows itself to be a flight from the world and its light, and in turn leads to suffocation. The writer digs into the depths,

A HUNGER ARTIST

believing he will rescue something buried, but that something may be himself. In doing so, he buries himself alive: "Weakling, it is not true that you are buried in the mine and the masses of rock separate you from the world and its light, rather you are outside and want to reach the person buried, and are weak before the stones, and the world and its light make you more weaker still. And at every instant, the one you wish to rescue is suffocating, and you must work like a madman, and he will never suffocate, and you never will be permitted to leave off with your work."[3]

Kafka's primary relation to the world is fear. This makes any serenity before the world impossible. His fear of death is reflected in everything. He is afraid of change or of travel. Life, which is nothing but the lighting up of a corpse, is condemned to a deadly numbness. The writer confines himself to a vicious circle of death: he fears death, because he has not lived, and he does not live, because he takes life to be the lighting up of a corpse.

Kafka's image of the writer is ambivalent. The writer is both *Homo doloris* and *Homo delectionis*. He does not renounce pleasure in its entirety. Writing remains a "sweet" reward for the devil's work—sweeter, possibly, than life, which he abandons. The writer is a "a construct of sensuality," which "continually buzz[es] about one's own or even another's form—and feast[s] on him." He gives himself over to the enjoyment of the beautiful: "That is your writer for you ... I sit here in the comfortable posture of the writer, ready for all sorts of fine things."

The writer is also a construct of self-indulgence. He mourns *himself*, he crowns *himself* with a wreath. With *sweet* tears, he nourishes his corpse: The writer "dies (or rather he does not live) and continually mourns himself." Instead of inhabiting the world, he inhabits *himself*. Self-centeredness, pathological clinging to the self, makes life impossible: "What is essential to life is only to forgo complacency." A deep regret at not having lived takes Kafka repeatedly in its clutches: "I could live and I do not live." Nor is regret free from self-indulgence: "But then why this sense of repining, this repining that never ceases? To make oneself finer and more savory? That is a part of it."

It is inevitably a question of enjoyment, of one's own enjoyment or the enjoyment of others. The writer is, as he states elsewhere, someone who must suffer on the behalf of "mankind." He is a martyr. He places the entire guilt of mankind on himself alone. On mankind's behalf, he takes up the cross. At the same time, makes sin pleasurable: "He is the scapegoat of mankind. He makes it possible for men to enjoy sin without guilt, almost without guilt." We must recollect that the writer is a "construct of sensuality." The imperative to sensuality brings writer and humanity together.

Addressing Kafka's theory of the writer, Max Brod responds:

> Your remarks concerning the writer—well, despite our friendship, the two of us plainly belong to different sorts. By writing, you console yourself for some negativity, be it real or merely imagined, in any case something you feel to be negative in life. But at least you can write amid unhappiness. For me, happiness and

writing hang by the same thread. If it breaks (and how weak it is!), I grow miserable. And when this occurs, I should rather strangle myself than write. You will say: writing is your way of strangling yourself and so on. But that is not a parallel. For this method of strangling oneself is the very one that is unknown to me. And I can only write when I am in a state of great spiritual equilibrium. Naturally it is never so great that writing becomes indispensable to me. It is here that you and I meet.[4]

Kafka replies that his relationship to writing and happiness is utterly different, that he flees happiness in order to write: "And certainly there is this difference, that I, should I ever have been happy, outside of writing and whatever is connected with it (I don't rightly know if I ever was)—at such times I was incapable of writing, with the result that everything had barely begun when the whole applecart tipped over, for the longing to write was always uppermost. This does not mean that I am fundamentally, innately, and honorably a writer by nature."[5] His renunciation of happiness is not "honorable," for he swears off happiness for a higher pleasure known as writing. His pleasure-seeking even capitalizes on his corpse. His fear of death may well derive from the radical distinction between death and pleasure-seeking: "My life was sweeter than other people's and my death will be more terrible by the same degree." Seen in this way, there exists no fundamental difference between a writing based on the "negative" and a writing that merges entirely with happiness. The writer *fasts* for writing, which promises a higher pleasure. He gives himself over fanatically to fasting, to hunger.

Kafka's "A Hunger Artist" is a passion narrative of the author. The story begins with a diagnosis of the times: "During these last decades the interest in professional fasting has markedly diminished." We live in an era with less and less interest in the passion for hunger, indeed, *in any passion whatsoever*. And yet the passion of the "martyr" of hunger is not a pure suffering, for the renunciation of nourishment brings him *happiness*: "For he alone knew, what no other initiate knew, how easy it was to fast. It was the easiest thing in the world. He made no secret of this, yet people did not believe him, at the best they set him down as modest, most of them, however, thought he was out for publicity." The hunger artist suffers most from the eternal necessity of extinguishing his hunger too early. His weakness after a period of starvation is simply "a consequence of the premature ending of his fast." The fasting period is determined by the demands of publicity alone. Advertising takes precedence over passion. It is even suggested to the hunger artist that he is "out for publicity." What matters above all is to arouse the attention of "the public": "The longest period of fasting was fixed by his impresario at forty days, beyond that term he was not allowed to go, not even in great cities, and there was good reason for it, too. Experience had proved that for about forty days the interest of the public could be stimulated by a steadily increasing pressure of advertisement, but after that the town began to lose interest, sympathetic support began notably to fall off; there were of course local variations as between one town and another or one country and another, but as a general rule forty days marked the limit." The passion for hunger *as entertainment* obeys the dictates of publicity.

The interest of the "amusement seekers" wanes progressively. The lack of enthusiasm for the passion of hunger, for passion in general, sends the hunger artist packing to a circus. In a cage next to the animals, the martyr, the hunger artist, lives out his meager existence, until here, too, he ends up entirely forgotten. No more interest exists in the passion of hunger: "People grew familiar with the strange idea that they could be expected, in times like these, to take an interest in a hunger artist, and with this familiarity the verdict went out against him. He might fast as much as he could, and he did so; but nothing could save him now, people passed him by. Just try to explain to anyone the art of fasting!" His cage, the locus of his passion, is now no more than "an impediment on the way to the menagerie":

> An overseer's eye fell on the cage one day and he asked the attendants why this perfectly good cage should be left standing there unused with dirty straw inside it; nobody knew, until one man, helped out by the notice board, remembered about the hunger artist. They poked into the straw with sticks and found him in it. "Are you still fasting?" asked the overseer, "when on earth do you mean to stop?" "Forgive me, everybody," whispered the hunger artist; only the overseer, who had his ear to the bars, understood him. "Of course," said the overseer, and tapped his forehead with a finger

to let the attendants know what state the man was in, "we forgive you." "I always wanted you to admire my fasting," said the hunger artist. "We do admire it," said the overseer, affably. "But you shouldn't admire it," said the hunger artist. "Well then we don't admire it," said the overseer, "but why shouldn't we admire it?" "Because I have to fast, I can't help it," said the hunger artist. "What a fellow you are," said the overseer, "and why can't you help it?" "Because," said the hunger artist, lifting his head a little and speaking, with his lips pursed, as if for a kiss, right into the overseer's ear, so that no syllable might be lost, "because I couldn't find the food I liked. If I had found it, believe me, I should have made no fuss and stuffed myself like you or anyone else."

His hunger art is revealed to be an *art of negativity*. It refuses *all* nourishment. It says *no* to all that *is*. But this negativity does not occasion pure suffering. Instead, it forms the basis of his happiness. The hunger artist is "too fanatically devoted to fasting."

With this enigmatic confession, the passion tale of the hunger artist ends. He is buried along with his straw. His post is taken over by a young panther. Its entry into the cage brings great relief to all, "even the most insensitive felt it refreshing." The well-nourished animal furnishes an antithesis to the hunger-martyr, even to *passion* itself. Sovereign joy for life streams from his throat: "The food he liked was brought him without hesitation by the attendants; he seemed not even to miss his freedom; his noble body, furnished almost to the bursting point with all that it needed, seemed to carry freedom around with it too; somewhere in his jaws it seemed to lurk; and the joy of life streamed with such ardent passion from his throat that for the onlookers it was not easy to stand the shock of it. But they braced themselves, crowded around the cage, and did not want ever to move away." The "amusement-seekers" now rush toward the beast, pleased to see this new spectacle at the *circus*. They identify themselves with its complacent joy for life, which roars with a powerful glow from the throat of the animal. The hedonistic affirmation of life offers a rest from the *passion for negation*.

Both the hedonistic animal and the hunger artist live out their existence in captivity. But this does not appear to exclude the possibility of happiness. Perhaps it even takes it as a given. The young panther is an illustration of happiness without passion, of sovereign joy in life. That freedom which lurks somewhere in his teeth is undoubtedly strange or absurd. But the freedom of the hunger martyr, that is, the freedom of negation, is no less problematic. And the happiness of the hedonistic beast, which corresponds to the pleasure of digestion, is no more illusory or deceptive than the happiness of negation.

Art as passion is perhaps always a hunger art, concealing a certain pleasure the annihilation of that which *is*. For this reason, the hunger martyr receives a "sweet and wonderful reward" for the negativity of his existence. The hunger artist and the hedonistic animal are not fundamentally different from one another. The imperative to happiness binds them in their depths.

SERENITY BEFORE THE WORLD

Good entertainment is one of the means man turns to in order to forget the absence of God.

George Steiner's concept of art leaves no room for doubt. Art is transcendence and metaphysics. At its core, it is religious. It brings us "in sane touch" with that which "transcends."[1] It is the "making formal of epiphany." With it, "there is a shining through."[2] Every art possessing "compelling stature"—Steiner mentions Kafka explicitly—is a "referral" to "a transcendent dimension ... which is felt to reside either explicitly, this is to say ritually, theologically, by force of revelation—or implicitly, outside immanent and purely secular reach."[3] A "mantic breath of strangeness" inhabits art.[4] Inevitably an "otherness" adheres to it, an "aura of terror."[5] Art allows us to sense that we are "neighbors to the unknown."[6]

For Steiner too, *art is passion*. Passion alone grants access to transcendence: "Whether we would or not, these overwhelming, commonplace inexplicabilities and the imperative of questioning which is the core of man make us close neighbors to the transcendent. Poetry, art, music are the medium of that neighborhood."[7] The artist is *Homo doloris*. The "apprehensions and figurations in the play of metaphysical imagining, in the poem and the music," tell, according to Steiner, "of pain and of hope, of the flesh which is said to taste of ash." The grief of ashes is the motive force of art. All artistic forms of expression are *forms of passion*. They "have risen out of an immensity of waiting."[8] True art as passion remains mindful of death. Its "seriousness" is owed to being-toward-death. Heroic resistance to mortality distinguishes art as passion. Entertainment, in contrast, is immanence. It is not freighted with metaphysical potential. It is ephemeral and doomed.

Regarding the theologization of art, Theodor Adorno stands near to Steiner, though his own thinking displays far more nuance. Despite Adorno's inclination toward *absolute passion*, he recognizes a certain point of convergence of art and entertainment. To cite him once more: "Amusement, free of all restraint, would be not only the opposite of art but its complementary extreme." Where entertainment liberates itself toward passion, it bends toward art. Not only the theological elevation of art lacks *serenity*, but also, in equal measure, the theological liberation of entertainment. Pure sense and pure nonsense converge in hysteria.

Art history is not necessarily a passion narrative. Pain, fear, solitude—these are not the only motivations for the production of art forms. The presence of art need not consist in referral to transcendence. The *art of immanence* and the *art of the ephemeral* are not contradictions in terms. Both are animated by a wholly different relationship to death and finitude whose expression is neither the pale reflection of the lit corpse nor heroic resistance to death. Kafka's death-passion must give way to conscious innocence. In a conversation, Robert Rauschenberg clarifies his relationship to death: "*Barbara Rose*: In all your imagery, there is no death. ... It's interesting that in all your years of producing new directions in your art, you have never gotten into death imagery. Is that something you ever think about? *Robert Rauschenberg*: Not often. I have always said that life has nothing to do with death. They're two separate things, and that's the way it ought to be. If that's innocent, so be it. Innocence is not like virginity. Virginity you can only have once. Innocence you have to nourish every day."[9]

For Rauschenberg, art is not defined outside the world, "outside immanent and purely secular reach." His art is one of *immanence*. It does not withdraw from the world. A calm friendliness, an "affection" toward the world distinguishes his art: "The next thing is affection. Even though it's just an old piece of can, that doesn't stop me from falling in love with it."[10] Rauschenberg's art of immanence inhabits, adorns, transfigures the quotidian, the ephemeral, the transitory. If his art is religious, then it is a religion of immanence or the quotidian. It discovers the spirituality of the everyday, of the inconspicuous, of the ephemeral. The artist rummages through the world, attends lovingly on everyday things, and tells *their* story: "I like the experience that says a shirt changes when it gets in the sun a little, or when you go swimming in it, or when the dog sleeps on it. I like the history of objects."[11] Rauschenberg distances himself repeatedly from transcendent art and from its metaphysical-religious pathos. That *passion for truth* that characterizes Barnett Newman is foreign to him. According to Newman, the task of art consists of wresting "truth from the void."[12]

Art is *life.* Life means, as Kafka rightly says, renouncing "complacency." It is thus a matter of avoiding the reproduction of the ego: "I don't want my personality to come out through the piece. That's why I keep the television on all the time. And I keep the windows open."[13] Rauschenberg leaves the window open so that no monadic inwardness may seal off his view of the world. The television de-*internalizes* the ego, *deflects* it toward the world. It *dispassions* the individual. It is in a sense an instrument of primordial distraction. We are deflected from ourselves and toward the world. Rauschenberg's use of the television is plainly a spiritual one. Art is expressly a *deviation toward the world.* Open windows counteract monadic absorption in *worldless inwardness.* Art is not necessarily the product of an undistracted life fixated on death. Rauschenberg comments, *pace* those artists who only paint nightmares, who only inhabit and adorn their own inwardness: "My attitude is that if I am in a working situation, I just look around and see what's around me. If I've picked up something, touched something or moved somewhere, then something starts happening."[14] This is a deflection from the ego to *things in one's surroundings.* This deviation also extends to the body: "I want to free my body, my head and my thoughts from my ego."[15] This is the freedom that Kafka fails to achieve: "I have not bought myself off by my writing. I died my whole life long and now I will really die."[16] Even the fear of death that plagued Kafka is connected with a hypertrophy of the ego: "I need to be free from my fears also. In this way all the energy that physically creates can move freely. I think fears are the same as ego. Perhaps they're cousins."[17]

Less ego means less world. And less fear means greater serenity. Rauschenberg's relaxed relationship to entertainment is based on *serenity before the world:* "I love television and I always keep it on. I don't like it when people are always changing the stations and interrupting the shows. I'd rather watch a lousy show all the way through."[18] Rauschenberg is at pains to suggest here that entertainment also belongs to the world, that television *too* is a window onto the world, and that he leaves it running, just as he leaves the window open, to countenance entertainment without succumbing to it. His creed is *to exclude nothing:* "*Barbara Rose*: You really have a desire to try and see and include everything. *Robert Rauschenberg*: I think that's what everything is about. *Barbara Rose*: But there is a desire to not shut anything out. Everything has to be brought into it—inclusion and not exclusion."[19] To be friendly also means "to include everything." The motto of Rauschenberg's art is: To offer a *friendly reception* to the world and its things. Art as passion, on the other hand, is highly selective or exclusive. No friendliness is proper to it. Rauschenberg's *art of friendliness* opens up another world, another *everydayness* that eschews both the art of passion and the art of entertainment. Neither passion nor entertainment is aware of friendly *circumspection*. Both are prisoners to blindness. They are unfamiliar with *serene friendliness to the world*.

Rauschenberg's art of friendliness takes *part* in the world. It is *one of* the possible means of access to the world. Art does not in the least take precedence here. Television, as a window onto the world, is also a means of access, and Rauschenberg always leaves it open. TV shows, too, *contain the world.* Against Heidegger, Rauschenberg would object that television does not necessarily signify a poverty of world, that Heidegger's own world is characterized by a kind of poverty, that it excludes a great deal, that a certain foreignness to the world motivates Heidegger's thinking, that Heidegger is ignorant of *serenity before the world.* Even after fifteen years, his relationship to television has not fundamentally changed. Only death, which has crept closer, provokes unease in him: "There's a television in almost every room, and they are all on 24 hours a day ... I just need them. If they all gave out, that would be almost like death. I would be cut off from everything. Then all I would have left is art."[20]

A METATHEORY OF ENTERTAINMENT

Enjoy *DIE ZEIT*.
—*Die Zeit*

What, then, is entertainment? How shall we account for its apparently infinite capacity for incorporation: "info-tainment, edutainment, servotainment, confrotainment, docu-drama"?[1] What does this ever-protean hybrid format of entertainment call forth? Is entertainment, which is talked about so much today, actually a long-familiar phenomenon that for some reason has become significant again even though it offers nothing new? One study states: "You can twist it and interpret it as you like: people like to be entertained—alone, with others, about others, and about God and the world, and they are very keen on adventure stories, colorful images, rousing music, and all kinds of games—in brief: on *communication lite*, and non-compulsory participation without high expectations or rules. Presumably it has always been this way and will continue to be as long as we are programmed for pleasure and sociability."[2] Does the ubiquity of entertainment today indicate a noteworthy process, a unique experience previously unavailable? Does it mark the appearance of something extraordinary that distinguishes or explains *the present day*? "Everything entertainment—enough said."[3] But it is not so clear—indeed, it is as far as possible from clear that everything ought now to be entertainment. What is happening here? Can we speak of some kind of paradigm shift?

Recently, there have been frequent attempts to grasp entertainment conceptually. But something about entertainment stubbornly resists conceptual markers. Hence a certain cluelessness pervades attempts to define it. This difficulty cannot simply be sidestepped with resort to history: "Often it is fruitful to start with the historical development, which many times proves more revealing than starting with a definition. Like so many other phenomena, entertainment has its origins in the eighteenth century, because only in the eighteenth century did the work and leisure time distinction in the modern sense come to exist."[4] The nobility had no need of entertainment because it pursued no regular form of work. Noble amusements, such as concerts or theater performances, were "more social activities than entertainments." No regular work means no leisure time. According to this thesis, entertainment is an activity employed to fill free time. But this *is* a definition of entertainment, and it is only thanks to this implicit definition that the phenomenon's apparent historical factuality takes shape. This historicization, meant to render a definition superfluous, is paradoxically preceded by a definition. More convincing, or *at least* free of contradictions, is the thesis that entertainment has always existed, from time immemorial: "The Greeks not only acted in theater, but also, like Penelope's suitors, played light music on the lyre; and Nausicaa delighted with her friends playing ball while

A METATHEORY OF ENTERTAINMENT

the waves washed Odysseus up on the shore. Medieval royal residences not only housed cloisters, but gave shelter to jesters."[5] The assertion that the Greeks and Romans were unfamiliar with entertainment because there was no separation of work and leisure time in their day makes little sense.

The ubiquity of entertainment is not simply the result of the constant expansion of free time, nor does this expansion of free time make entertainment more significant. The salient aspect of present-day entertainment is instead how far it oversteps the phenomenon of free time. Edutainment, for example, is not primarily related to the realm of free time. The ubiquity of entertainment expresses itself through a totalization that dissolves the division between work and free time. Even neologisms like *labotainment* or *theotainment* no longer appear oxymoronic. Morality could be conceived of as *allotainment*, with all this leading to a *culture of inclinations*. Historicization—locating entertainment in the eighteenth century—actually misses entirely the *historical* particularity of the *present-day* entertainment phenomenon.

The ubiquity of entertainment has recently become a commonplace: "The strangely scintillating, unclear concept 'entertainment' is first of all a neutral and open concept. Information can be entertaining, as can knowledge, work, even the world itself."[6] To what degree can the world itself be entertaining? Is this the declaration of a new understanding of the world or reality? Does the dazzle or the blurriness of the entertainment concept point toward factors that could lead to the totalization of entertainment? When even work itself must be entertaining, entertainment breaks its relationship to free time as a historical phenomenon rooted in the eighteenth century. Entertainment is now far more than an activity for killing free time. Even *cognitainment* is now conceivable. Such a hybrid marriage of knowledge and entertainment is not necessarily limited to free time, but instead bears an entirely novel relationship to knowledge. *Cognitainment* is opposed to *knowledge as passion*, to knowledge transfigured, theologized, even teleologized into an end in itself.

For Luhmann, too, entertainment is only "a component of modern leisure culture, charged with the function of destroying superfluous time."[7] In conceptualizing entertainment, Luhmann takes as his model the game. Entertainment is like a game; it consists of "episodes," conceiving of one part of reality as a time-bound game cordoned off from normal reality as a whole: "They are not transitions to another way of living. People are only preoccupied with them from time to time, without being able to relinquish other opportunities or to shed other burdens. ... The game always contains, in each of its operations, references to the real reality which exists at the same time. With every move it marks itself as a game; and it can collapse at any moment if things suddenly get serious. The cat jumps onto the chessboard."[8] Luhmann, too, overlooks distinctive aspects of the entertainment phenomena of today. Entertainment at present strains against all temporal and functional limitations. It is no longer "episodic," but is instead becoming *chronic*. It no longer affects only free time, but *time itself*. There is no difference between cat and chessboard. Even the cat is subordinate to the game. Behind the ubiquity of entertainment stands, in all probability, its creeping totalization. If this is so, then entertainment is currently giving rise to a new "lifestyle," a new *experience of world and time* that transcends the *episodic*.

According to Luhmann, a system constructs its own truth with the aid of a binary code. The distinction *true/untrue*, for example, is constitutive of the system of science. The binary code decides what *really* is. The system of mass media, which includes news and publicity as well as entertainment, functions via the binary code of *information/non-information*. "Each of these strands uses the information/non-information code, even if they use very different versions of it; but they differ in terms of the criteria which underpin the selection of information."[9] Entertainment selects information according to criteria distinct from news or publicity. Still, the binary code of information/non-information is generally speaking too vague to elucidate the particular nature of entertainment or even the mass media, because information is, as Luhmann affirms, constitutive of *communication as a whole* rather than being a specific property of mass media. *All* communication presupposes the selection, diffusion, and comprehension of information. Conceived as a mere subsidiary domain of mass media, entertainment is consigned to a marginal existence. For this reason, Luhmann fails to grasp, let alone illuminate, entertainment's ubiquity, which extends far past the domain of mass media.

To take one example, edutainment transcends the system of mass media beneath which Luhmann subsumes entertainment, belonging properly to the system of pedagogy. At present, entertainment seems to attach itself to every social system and to modify these systems so that each engenders its own forms of entertainment. Infotainment blurs the division between news and entertainment as subdomains of mass media. Luhmann's systems theory is incapable of grasping these hybrid formats. Edutainment breaks with the "fictional closure" that would distinguish it from the news. Nor is the "external frame" that signals the presence of entertainment, of a game, always clearly present.[10] The world itself will probably become a chessboard. The jumping cat will then be merely a *toy*. True, the "screen" is a framing device that categorizes feature films as entertainment; but it also projects news. The similarity of the external frame alone leads to a mingling of entertainment and news. Similarly, the line between "real reality" and the "fictional reality" of entertainment is increasingly vague. Entertainment has long laid claim to "real reality." It is now changing the social system as a whole, though without drawing attention to its own presence. A *hypersystem*, coextensive with the world, appears to be arising. The binary code of *entertaining/not entertaining* that lies at its basis will determine what is and is not *fit for the world*—indeed, even simply what *is*.

Entertainment has been raised to a new paradigm, to a new formula of world and being. In order to *be*, in order to belong to the *world*, it is necessary to be entertaining. Only the entertaining is *real* or *true*. The distinction between fictional and real reality, which Luhmann's concept of entertainment cleaves to, is no longer relevant. *Reality* itself appears to be an *effect* of entertainment.

For the spirit of passion, the totalization of entertainment may bear the marks of decadence. At heart, however, passion and entertainment are kin. The present study points to multiple examples of their hidden convergences. It is no coincidence that Kafka's hunger artist, as a figure of passion, and his hedonistic beast inhabit the same cage, despite their distinct relation to being and freedom. They remain two circus figures, *trading places until the end of time.*

NOTES

SWEET CROSS

1. Christian Gerber, *Historie der Kirchen-Ceremonien in Sachsen* (Dresden, 1732), 284.

2. Gerber, *Historie*, 283.

3. Cited in Martin Geck, *Johann Sebastian Bach: Mit Selbstzeugnissen und Bilddsokumenten* (Reinbek: Rowohlt, 1993), 77.

4. Wilibald Gurlitt, *Johann Sebastian Bach* (Kassel: Bärenreiter, 1947), 54.

5. Gerber, *Historie*, 282.

6. Gerber, 289.

7. Gerber, 279.

8. Gerber, 279.

9. Gerber, 279.

10. Gerber, 285.

11. Gerber, 288–289.

12. Cf. Christian Bunners, *Kirchenmusik und Seelenmusik: Studien zu Frömmigkeit und Musik im Luthertum des 17. Jahrhunderts* (Göttingen: Vanderhoek und Ruprecht, 1966), 65.

13. Bunners, *Kirchenmusik* , 129.

14. Gudrun Busch and Wolfgang Miersemann, eds., *Geistreicher Gesang: Halle und das pietistische Lied* (Tübingen: Franckesche Stiftungen, 1997), 205.

15. Teophi Großgebauer, *Drey Geistreiche Schriften: Wächterstimme aus dem verwüsteten Zion*, vol. 1 (Frankfurt, 1710), 215.

16. Großgebauer, *Drey Geistreiche Schriftten*, 192.

17. Großgebauer, 191.

18. [There is an untranslatable play on words here between *Gott* and *Ergötzung*.–Trans.]

19. Busch and Miersemann, *Geistreicher Gesang*, 102.

20. Emil Platen draws attention to the "unusual fact" that Bach had written the name of the librettist in cursive letters on the title page of his score. Emil Platen, *Die Matthäus-Passion von Johann Sebastian Bach* (Kassel: Bärenreiter, 1991, 72).

21. Rochus Freiherr von Liliencron, *Allgemeine Deutsche Biographie*, vol. 11 (Leipzig, 1880), 784.

22. [It should be noted that many scholars doubt the authenticity of this document. See Thomas Braatz, "The Problematical Origins of the *Generalbaßlehre* of 1738" (2012), https://www.bach-cantatas.com/Articles/GBLehre.pdf.—Trans.]

23. *Bach-Dokumente*, vol. 1, ed. the Bach Archive in Leipzig (Kassel: 1963), 334.

24. Friedrich Erhard Niedt, *The Musical Guide*, trans. Pamela L. Poulin and Imogen C. Taylor (Oxford: Clarendon Press, 1989) [translation slightly modified to clarify connections to Han's text.—Trans.].

25. [I have chosen this slightly odd formulation because *wort-arm* contains echoes of Heidegger's *weltarm*: "poor in world."—Trans.]

26. See Platen, *Die Matthäus-Passion*, 218.

27. See Martin Geck, *Die Wiederentdeckung der Matthäuspassion im 19. Jahrhundert: Die zeitgenössischen Dokumente und ihre ideengeschichtliche Deutung* (Regensburg: Bosse, 1967, 40).

28. Friedrich Nietzsche, *Briefe*, vol. 1 (New York: De Gruyter, 1977), 120.

29. See Friedrich Nietzsche, *Human, All Too Human: A Book for Free Spirits*, trans. R. J. Hollingdale (Cambridge: Cambridge University Press, 1939), 344–345.

30. Friedrich Nietzsche, *Jugendschriften*, vol. 1 (Munich: DTV, 1994), 26–27.

31. [Here Han employs the adjective *Heiter* and the noun *Heiterkeit*, which Nietzsche's translators have rendered in a number of ways, from "cheerfulness" to "serenity." I have chosen "gaiety" because of its strong association with Nietzsche's *Gay Science* and because Joan Stambaugh uses the same term in her translation of *Being and Time*, which I quote from here.—Trans.]

32. Friedrich Nietzsche, *Basic Writings of Nietzsche*, trans. Walter Kaufmann (New York: Random House, 1992), 616.

33. Nietzsche, *Basic Writings*, 613–614.

34. Friedrich Nietzsche, *Nachgelassene Fragmente 1885–1887: Kritische Studienausgabe*, vol. 12 (New York: De Gruyter, 1988), 344, 361.

35. Friedrich Nietzsche, *Nachgelassene Fragmente 1887–1889, Kritische Studienausgabe*, vol. 13 (New York: De Gruyter, 1988), 496.

36. *Plato: The Collected Dialogues, Including the Letters*, ed. Edith Hamilton and Huntington Cairns (Princeton: Princeton University Press, 1961), 1301.

37. The tender turn of phrase "Good night, my Jesus" and the German diminutive "Jesulein" ("O Jesulein süß," Bach, *Schemelli Gesangbuch*, BWV 493) testify to the presence of a religious inclination toward kitsch. See Ludwig Giesz, *Phänomenologie des Kitsches* (Munich: Fink, 1971), 45: "Religious kitsch offers a veritable goldmine for the kitsch's ingenuity, which confronts the most transcendent realities—God, the saints—not with a numinous frisson, but with groveling sentimentality. God, the wholly other, becomes 'dear God,' 'sweet Jesus,' 'gentle baby Jesus.'"

BUTTERFLY DREAMS

1. Heinrich Heine, *Reisebilder: Historisch-kritische Gesamtausgabe* (Hamburg: Hoffmann and Campe, 1986), 48. An English version of this text is available in Peter Wortsmann's translation, published by Archipelago Books.

2. Robert Schumann, *Gesammelte Schriften über Musik und Musiker*, vol. 1 (Leipzig: Georg Wigands Verlag, 1914), 127.

3. E. T. A. Hoffmann, *Schriften zur Musik* (Munich: Winkler, 1977), 366.

4. Amadeus Wendt, *Rossinis Leben und Treiben* (Leipzig, 1824), 394–395.

5. Richard Wagner, *Publikum und Popularität: Gesammelte Schriften und Dichtungen in zehn Bänden*, vol. 10 (Berlin: Bong and Co., 1914), 76.

6. Wagner, *Publikum*, 75–76.

7. Richard Wagner, *Oper und Drama: Gesammelte Schriften*, vol. 3 (Berlin: Bong and Co., 1914), 280.

8. Wagner, *Oper*, 255. Bernd Sponheur examines the Beethoven–Rossini controversy in depth in his monograph *Musik als Kunst und Nicht-Kunst: Untersuchungen zur Dichotomie von "hoher" und "niederer" Musik im musikästhetischen Denken zwischen Kant und Hanslick* (Kassel: Bärenreiter, 1987).

9. Wagner, *Oper*, 312.

10. Arthur Schopenhauer, *The Word as Will and Representation*, trans. Judith Norman, Alistair Welchman, and Christopher Janaway (Cambridge: Cambridge University Press, 2010), 289.

11. Wendt, *Rossinis Leben*, 324.

12. Wendt, 327. In his autobiography, Grillparzer recalls that Rossini had resolved to stop composing, among other reasons because there was no longer anyone capable of singing.

13. Wendt, 325.

14. Wendt, 343.

15. Wendt, 237–238.

16. Wendt, 342.

17. Georg Wilhelm Friedrich Hegel,. *Briefe*, vol. 3 (Hamburg: Meiner, 1954), 65.

18. Georg Wilhelm Friedrich Hegel, *Vorlesungen über die Ästhetik III: Werke in zwanzig Bänden*, vol. 15 (Frankfurt: Suhrkamp, 1970), 210.

19. Georg Wilhelm Friedrich Hegel, *Aesthetics: Lectures on Fine Art*, vol. 1, trans. T. M. Knox (Oxford: Clarendon Press, 1975), 7.

20. Hegel, *Aesthetics*, 10.

21. Hegel, 10.

22. Hegel, 11.

23. Hegel, *Briefe*, 73–74.

24. Georg Wilhelm Friedrich Hegel, *Jenaer kritische Schriften: Werke in zwanzig Bänden*, vol. 2 (Frankfurt: Suhrkamp, 1970), 128.

25. Hegel, *Briefe*, 71.

26. Friedrich Nietzsche, *The Gay Science*, trans. Walter Kaufmann (New York: Knopf Doubleday, 2010), 134.

27. [While I have referred here to the more properly English concepts of "art music" and "popular music," Theodor Adorno's terms in the original German, "E-Musik" (*ernste Musik* or "serious music") and "U-Musik" (*Unterhaltungsmusik*, "entertainment music"), should be kept in mind, as they clearly have import for Han's theses on entertainment.—Trans.]

28. Theodor Adorno, *Gesammelte Schriften*, vol. 19 (Frankfurt: Suhrkamp, 2004), 548.

ON LUXURY

1. Richard Wagner, *Oper und Drama: Gesammelte Schriften*, vol. 3 (Berlin: Bong and Co., 1914), 249–250.

2. Wagner, *Oper*, 260.

3. Wagner, 250.

4. Wagner, 60.

5. Wagner, 254.

6. Wagner, 158.

7. Wagner, 250.

8. Friedrich Nietzsche, *The Gay Science*, trans. Walter Kaufmann (New York: Knopf Doubleday, 2010), 134.

9. Wagner, *Oper*, 255.

10. Richard Wagner, *Das Kunstwerk der Zukunft: Gesammelte Schriften und Dichtungen*, vol. 3 (Berlin: Bong and Co., 1914), 48.

11. Wagner, *Kunstwerk* 44.

12. Wagner, 49.

13. Wagner, 50.

14. Wagner, 54.

15. Friedrich Nietzsche, *Nachgelassene Fragmente 1875–1879: Kritische Studienausgabe*, vol. 8 (New York: De Gruyter, 1988), 242.

16. Friedrich Nietzsche, *Morgenröthe: Kritische Studienausgabe*, vol. 3 (New York: De Gruyter, 1988), 253.

17. Friedrich Nietzsche, *Nachgelassene Fragmente 1875–1879: Kritische Studienausgabe*, vol. 9 (New York: De Gruyter, 1988), 152.

18. Theodor Adorno, *Mimimal Moralia*, trans. E. F. N. Jephcott (New York: Verso, 2005), 116.

19. Theodor Adorno and Max Horkheimer, *Dialectic of Enlightenment*, trans. Edmund Jephcott (Stanford: Stanford University Press, 2002), 113.

SATORI

1. See Bernd Sponheuer, *Musik als Kunst und Nicht-Kunst* (Kassel: Bärenreiter, 1987). Where art is appropriated by power or dominant interests, it undergoes hierarchization. But in Far Eastern culture, art cannot simply be overtaken by power and dominant interests. The Far Eastern idea of the beautiful is unsuited to the representation of power, as it does not promulgate a vision of the perfect or the unchangeable, unlike the Platonic idea of the beautiful. *Wabi*, a Japanese term for the experience of the beautiful, makes explicit reference to the unfinished, the transitory, or the fleeting. It designates as beautiful not the ripe cherry blossom, but the flowers at the moment of falling: "Were we to live on forever—were the dews of Adashino never to vanish, the smoke on Toribeyama never to fade away—then indeed would man not feel the pity of things. Truly the beauty of life is uncertainty." Yoshido Kenko, *Essays in Idleness*, trans. Sir George Bayley Sansom (New York: Cosimo Classics, 2009), 5. No holder of power would wish to be entirely identified with the transitory, fleeting appearance of the beautiful. The famed master of the tea ceremony Rikyu likewise remarks that the tea bowl should not look impeccable. He fails to understand those who are "irked at the smallest imperfection." See Paul H. Varley and Isao Kumakura, eds., *Tea in Japan: Essays on the History of Chanoyu* (Honolulu: University of Hawaii Press, 1995), 171–170.

2. *Haiku: Japanische Gedichte*, ed. and trans. Dietrich Krusche (Munich: dtv, 1994), 121: "Zen is inconceivable without haiku, nor is there a more valuable literary testament to Japanese Zen culture than haiku."

3. Sōkan (1394–1481), in *Haiku*, trans. Jan Ulenbrook (Stuttgart: Hayne Verlagn, 1995), 240.

4. Roland Barthes, *Empire of Signs* (New York: FSG, 1983), 78.

5. Barthes, *Empire*, 78. [In the German translation, Barthes speaks of *Glanz* or "splendor"; in the French original, however, the word is matité: matteness, flatness, duskiness.—Trans.]

6. Barthes, 82.

7. Barthes, 74.

8. Sōkan, trans. R. H. Blyth, quoted in Jack, "Haiku: A Whole Lot More than 5-7-5," tofugu.com, October 10, 2017, https://www.tofugu.com/japan/haiku/.

9. Teitoku, trans. Harold Gould Henderson, quoted in Jack, "Haiku."

10. Basho's famous Frog Haiku (*An old pond / a frog jumps in / sound of water*) is the product of a social gathering. If one listens to it closely, it has a humorous element. Nor does the following haiku by Basho point toward satori: "Fleas and lice / a horse pissing / by my pillow."

11. Peter Pörtner, "*Mono*—Über die paradoxe Verträglichkeit der Dinge: Anmerkungen zur Geschichte der Wahrnehmungen in Japan," in *Komparative Ästhetik: Künste und ästhetische Erfahrungen zwischen Asien und Europa.* ed. R. Eberfeld and G. Wohlfahrt (Cologne: edition chōra, 2000), 211–226. From page 217: "Japanese aesthetics is worldview and lifestyle. Art here is traditionally embedded in daily life to a far greater degree than in the West. It is hence perhaps not art at all in the pregnant, Western sense of the term."

12. The influence of Confucian morality on art in Japan was far weaker than in China or Korea. This accounts for the more intense aestheticization of the lived environment in Japan.

13. Chinese art rarely harbors social critique. See, e.g., Roger Goepper, *Vom Wesen chinesischer Malerei* (Munich: Prestel, 1962), 101.

14. Friedrich Schiller, "Gedanken über den Gebrauch des Gemeinen und Niedrigen in der Kunst," in *Sämtliche Werke*, vol. 5 (Munich: dtv, 1962), 537.

15. Richard Wagner, *Oper und Drama: Gesammelte Schriften*, vol. 3 (Berlin: Bong and Co., 1914), 255.

16. The production of erotic imagery was an economic mainstay for *ukiyo-e* painters and their printers. There were frequent prohibitions on erotic images, but the charge of obscenity was first leveled against them only in 1869, and even in that case, the cause lay with a rapid spread of Western moral conceptions. See Friedrich B. Schwan, *Handbuch japanischer Holzschnitt* (Munich: Iudicum, 2003), 528.

17. In the Edo period, *ukiyo-e* represented a common frame of mind. Not escape and renunciation, but joy in life and openness to pleasure were characteristic reactions to the fleeting and transitory. This hedonistic approach is evoked in Asai Ryoi's tale "Ukiyo Monogatari." *Ukiyo-zoōshi* is the name of the coarse entertainment literature illustrated by *ukiyo-e* artists. See Schwan, *Handbuch*, 89.

18. Joachim Gasquet, *Cézanne: A Memoir with Conversations* (London: Thames and Hudson, 1991).

19. Gasquet, *Cézanne*.

20. Gasquet.

21. Roger Goepper, *Meisterwerke des japanischen Farbenholzschnitts* (Graz: Adeva, 1973), 13.

22. Adalbert Stifter, *Werke und Briefe: Historisch-kritische Gesamtausgabe*, vol. 2 (Mainz: Kohlhammer, 1982), 9.

23. Theodor Adorno and Max Horkheimer, *Dialectic of Enlightenment*, trans. Edmund Jephcott (Stanford: Stanford University Press, 2002), 116. Adorno's critique of culture represents a blind negation of the extant. Every affirmation amounts to a capitulation of thinking. "The liberation which amusement promises," according to Adorno, "is from thinking as negation."

24. Li Po, quoted in Yuming Luo, *Concise History of Chinese Literature* (Leiden: Brill, 2011), 307.

25. Thomas Cleary and J. C. Cleary, *The Blue Cliff Record* (Boston: Shambala, 1977), 44.

26. Yunmen, *Zen-Worte vom Wolkentor-Berg* (Bern: O. W. Barth Bei Scherz, 1994), 105.

27. [Han cites one oft-repeated version. An earthier rendition can be found in Burton Watson's *Zen Teachings of Master Lin-chi* (New York: Cambridge University Press, 1999), 31: "Eat your rice, and if you get tired, then lie down. Fools may laugh at me, but wise men will know what I mean."—Trans.]

28. Quoted in D. T. Suzuki, *Essays in Zen Buddhism, Third Series* (New Delhi: Munshiram Manoharlal Publishers, 2000), 37–38.

MORAL ENTERTAINMENT

1. Immanuel Kant, *Critique of Practical Reason*, trans. Mary Gregor (Cambridge: Cambridge University Press, 1997), 29.

2. Kant, *Critique of Practical Reason*, 128.

3. Kant, 61.

4. Kant, 92.

5. Kant, 90.

6. Kant, 91.

7. Immanuel Kant, *Critique of Judgment*, trans. James Creed Meredith (Oxford: Oxford University Press, 1952), 101.

8. Kant, *Critique of Practical Reason*, 90.

9. Kant, *Critique of Practical Reason*, 122.

10. Julien Offray de La Mettrie, *Oeuvres philosophiques* (Paris, 1796), 165.

11. La Mettrie, *Oeuvres philosophiques*, 162. See also 184: "We see that the entire difference between the wicked and the good is that the former prefers individual to general interest, while the latter sacrifice their good for that of their fellow man or the public."

12. Kant, *Critique of Practical Reason*, 100.

13. *Der Glückselige: Eine moralische Wochenschrift*, Part 1 (Halle, 1763), 3.

14. See Wolfgang Martens, "Die Geburt des Journalisten in der Aufklärung," in *Wolfenbütteler Studien zur Aufklärung*, vol. 1, ed. G. Schulz (Bremen: Jacobi Verlag, 1974), 84–98, at 91: "The second half of the eighteenth century is the era of the charitable magazine, for readers' benefit and pleasure, as their inevitable philanthropic motto ran. Here, in addition to entertainment, general wisdom, and morality, writers offer practical recommendations, advice, tips, and prescriptions to serve the common good."

15. Cited in Wolfgang Martens, *Die Botschaft der Tugend: Die Aufklärung im Spiegel der deutschen Moralischen Wochenschriften* (Stuttgart: Metzler, 1968), 71.

16. Wolfgang Martens, ed., *Der Patriot: Nach der Originalausgabe Hamburg 1724–26 in drei Textbänden und einem Kommentarband kritisch herausgegeben*, vol. 1 (Berlin: de Gruyter, 1969), 7.

17. Cited in Martens, *Die Botschaft*, 272.

18. Dieter Petzold, "Die Lust am erhobenen Zeigefinger: Zur Dialektik von Unterhaltung und moralischer Belehrung, am Beispiel des Struwwelpeter," in *Unterhaltung: Sozial- und Literaturwissenschaftliche Beiträge zu ihren Formen und Funktionen* (Erlangen: Universitätsbund, 1994), 89.

19. Niklas Luhmann, *The Reality of Mass Media*, trans. Kathleen Cross (Stanford: Stanford University Press, 2000), 58.

20. [When Han speaks here of Kant's discussion of "moral conversation," the German term, "moralische Unterhaltung," is synonymous with "moral entertainment."—Trans.]

21. Kant, *Critique of Practical Reason*, 122.

22. Kant, 123.

23. Kant, 123.

24. Kant, 125.

25. Kant, 123.

26. Kant, 126.

27. Kant, 128.

28. Kant, 128.

29. Kant, 125.

30. Kant, 127.

HEALTHY ENTERTAINMENT

1. Kant, *Critique of Judgment*, trans. James Creed Meredith (Oxford: Oxford University Press), 162–163.

2. Kant, 159.

3. Kant. 163.

4. Kant, 115.

5. Kant, 135–136.

6. Kant, 121.

7. Kant, 38.

8. Kant, 161.

9. Kant, 162.

10. Kant, 161.

11. Kant, 160.

12. Kant, 162.

13. Kant, 160.

14. Kant, 163.

15. Kant, 104.

16. Kant, 161: "Suppose that someone tells the following story: An Indian at an Englishman's table in Surat saw a bottle of ale opened, and all the beer turned into froth and flowing out. The repeated exclamations of the Indian showed his great astonishment. 'Well, what is so wonderful in that?' asked the

Englishman. 'Oh, I'm not surprised myself,' said the Indian, 'at its getting out, but at how you ever managed to get it all in.' At this we laugh, and it gives us hearty pleasure."

17. Kant, 78.

18. Kant, 99.

19. Kant, 88.

20. Kant, 103–104.

21. Kant, 104.

22. Kant, 160.

23. Kant, 161.

24. Kant, *Critique of Judgement*, trans. and with notes by J. H. Bernard (London: Macmillan, 1892), 221.

25. Kant, *Critique of Judgment* (Meredith translation), 40.

26. [*Geschäft*, which translators of Kant render as "all we have to do," also means "business" or "trade."—Trans.]

27. Immanuel Kant, *Anthropology from a Pragmatic Point of View*, trans. Robert B. Lowden (Cambridge: Cambridge Univeristy Press, 2006), 130.

28. Kant, *Anthropology*, 130.

29. Kant, 131.

30. Kant, 127.

31. Immanuel Kant, *Metaphysics of Morals*, trans. Mary Gregor (Cambridge: Cambridge University Press, 1991), 274.

32. Immanuel Kant, *Religion and Rational Theology*, trans. Allan W. Wood (Cambridge: Cambridge University Press, 1996), 322.

33. Immanuel Kant, *Verkündigung des nahen Abschlusses eines Traktats zum ewigen Frieden in der Philosophie: Werke in 10 Bänden*, vol. 5 (Darmstadt: Wissenschaftliche Buchgesellschaft, 1983), 406–407.

34. Kant, *Verkündigung*, 407.

BEING AS PASSION

1. Peter Glotz, "Über die Vertreibung der Langeweile oder Aufklärung und Massenkultur," in *Die Zukunft der Aufklärung* (Frankfurt: Suhrkamp, 1988), 217.

2. Martin Heidegger, *Being and Time*, trans. Joan Stambaugh (Albany: SUNY Press, 1996), 357.

3. Heidegger, *Being and Time*, 242.

4. Heidegger, 242.

5. Heidegger, 165.

6. *Earnest*, related to the German *ernst*, derives from the Proto-Germanic *ernustuz*, meaning "struggle" or "fight."

7. Heidegger, *Being and Time*, 352.

8. Heidegger, 119.

9. Heidegger, 159.

10. Heidegger, 159.

11. Heidegger, 159.

12. Heidegger, 120.

13. Heidegger, 120.

14. Heidegger, 158.

15. Heidegger, 158–159.

16. Heidegger, 159.

17. Heidegger, 167.

18. Heidegger, 297.

19. Heidegger, 158.

20. Heidegger, 145.

21. Heidegger, 177.

22. Heidegger, 244.

23. Heidegger, 317.

24. Heidegger, 177.

25. Heidegger, 98.

26. Heidegger, 161.

27. [There is an untranslatable play on words here: *fern sehen*—"to see into the distance"; *fernsehen*—"to watch television"; *Fernseher*—"television." Below Han speaks of the radio as enabling a kind of *Fern-hören* or distance-hearing.—Trans.]

28. Heidegger, 98.

29. Martin Heidegger, *Discourse on Thinking*, trans. John M. Anderson and E. Hans Freund (New York: Harper and Row, 1966), 48.

30. Martin Heidegger, "Why Do I Stay in the Provinces?" in *Martin Heidegger: The Man and the Thinker*, ed. Thomas Sheehan (Piscataway, NJ: Transaction Publishers, 2009), 27.

31. Heidegger, "Why Do I Stay," 70.

32. Heidegger, 70.

33. Martin Heidegger, *Poetry, Language, Thought*, trans. Albert Hofstadter (New York: HarperCollins, 1971), 180. [Translation slightly modified to stress alliterative elements.—Trans.]

34. Martin Heidegger, *Bremer und Freiburger Vorträge: Gesamtausgabe*, vol. 79 (Frankfurt: Vittorio Klostermann, 1994), 66.

35. Martin Heidegger, *Contributions to Philosophy (From Enowning)*, trans. Parvis Emad and Kenneth Maly (Bloomington: Indiana University Press), 199, 292, 283.

36. Heidegger, *Bremer und Freiburger Vorträge*, 122.

37. Heidegger, "Why Do I Stay," 57.

38. Peter Handke, *A Journey to the Rivers: Justice for Serbia*, trans. Scott Abbott (New York: Viking, 1997), 30.

39. Hubert Winkels, *Leselust und Bildermacht. Literatur, Fernsehen und Neue Medien* (Cologne: Kiepenheuer & Witsch, 1997), 89–90.

40. Handke, *Journey*, 40 (translation modified).

41. Franz Kafka, *Letters to Milena*, trans. Philip Boehm (New York: Schocken, 1990), 229.

42. Kafka, *Letters to Milena*, 229. See also Kafka, *Letters to Friends, Family, and Editors*, trans. Richard and Clara Winston (New York: Schocken, 1977): "So if I do not write, that is due chiefly to 'strategic' reasons such as have become dominant for me in recent years. I do not trust words and letters, my words and letters; I want to share my heart with people but not with phantoms that play with the words and read the letters with slavering tongue. Especially I do not trust letters, and it is a strange belief that all one has to do is seal the envelope in order to have the letter reach the addressee safely." Kafka has a more human form of art in mind: "I forgot to add to my remark above: It sometimes seems to me that the nature of art in general, the existence of art, is explicable solely in terms of such 'strategic considerations,' of making possible the exchange of truthful words from person to person."

43. Heidegger, "Why Do I Stay," 70.

44. Heidegger, 70.

A HUNGER ARTIST

1. Franz Kafka, *Letters to Friends, Family, and Editors*, trans. Richard and Clara Winston (New York: Schocken, 1977).

2. Franz Kafka, *Nachgelassene Schriften und Fragmente II* (Frankfurt: Fischer, 1992), 355.

3. Kafka, *Nachgelassene Schriften*, 352.

4. Max Brod and Franz Kafka, *Eine Freundschaft: Briefwechsel*, vol. 2 (Frankfurt: Fischer, 1989), 381.

5. Kafka, *Letters to Friends, Family, and Editors*.

SERENITY BEFORE THE WORLD

1. George Steiner, *Real Presences* (London: Faber & Faber, 2010), 261.

2. Steiner, *Real Presences*, 260.

3. Steiner, 249.

4. Steiner, 243.

5. Steiner, 242.

6. Steiner, 260.

7. Steiner, 248.

8. Steiner, 268.

9. Barbara Rose and Robert Rauschenberg, *An Interview with Robert Rauschenberg* (New York: Vintage, 1983), 125.

10. Rose and Rauschenberg, *An Interview*, 121.

11. Rose and Rauschenberg , 96.

12. Barnett Newman, quoted in *Abstract Expressionism: Creators and Critics*, ed. Clifford Ross (New York: Abrahams Publishers, 1990), 126.

13. Rose and Rauschenberg, *An Interview*, 72.

14. Rose and Rauschenberg, 82.

15. Rose and Rauschenberg, 85.

16. Kafka, *Letters to Friends, Family, and Editors.*

17. Rose and Rauschenberg, *An Interview*, 85

18. Rose and Rauschenberg, 95.

19. Rose and Rauschenberg, 75.

20. "Ich habe meinen Himmel," interview with Robert Rauschenberg in *Die Zeit*, January 12, 2006.

A METATHEORY OF ENTERTAINMENT

1. Joachim Westerbarkey, "Von allerley Kurzweyl oder vom wissenschaftlichen Umgang mit einem antiquierten Begriff," in *a/effektive Kommunikation: Unterhaltung und Werbung*, ed. Siegfried J. Schmidt, Joachim Westerbarkey, and Guido Zurstiege (Munster: LIT, 2003), 21.

2. Westerbarkey, "Von allerley Kurzweyl," 13.

3. Peter Vorderer, "Was wissen wir über Unterhaltung?" in *a/ effektive Kommunikation*, 111.

4. Westerbarkey, "Von allerley Kurzweyl," 13.

5. Hans Thomas, "Was scheidet Unterhaltung von Information," in *Medienlust und Mediennutz. Unterhaltung als öffentliche Kommunikation*, ed. Louis Bosshart and Wolfgang Hoffmann-Riehm (Munich: UVK Verlag, 1994), 71.

6. Thomas, "Was scheidet Unterhaltung," 70.

7. Niklas Luhmann, *The Reality of Mass Media*, trans. Kathleen Cross (Stanford: Stanford University Press, 2000), 51.

8. Luhmann, *Reality of Mass Media*, 51–52.

9. Luhmann, 24.

10. Luhmann, 52.